the book of children

Also by Osho

Emotional Wellness
The Book of Understanding
Autobiography of a Spiritually Incorrect Mystic
The Book of Secrets
Pharmacy for the Soul
Love, Freedom, Aloneness
Meditation: The First and Last Freedom
Sex Matters
Your Answers Questioned
Osho Zen Tarot
Tao: The Pathless Path
Zen: The Path of Paradox
Yoga: The Science of the Soul
Tarot in the Spirit of Zen
Meditation for Busy People
Body Mind Balancing
Learning to Silence the Mind

AUDIO

Book of Secrets: Keys to Love and Meditation
Ah, This!
The Heart Sutra
TAO: The Three Treasures
Osho Meditations on Buddhism
Osho Meditations on Tantra
Osho Meditations on Tao
Osho Meditations on Yoga
Osho Meditations on Zen

the book of children

supporting the freedom and intelligence of
a new generation

OSHO

St. Martin's Griffin
New York

contents

the book of children

I

the qualities of the child

It is the child's experience that haunts intelligent people their whole life. They want it again—the same innocence, the same wonder, the same beauty. It is now a faraway echo; it seems as if you have seen it in a dream.

But the whole of religion is born out of the haunting childhood experience of wonder, of truth, of beauty, of life in its beautiful dance all around. In the songs of the birds, in the colors of the rainbows, in the fragrance of the flowers the child goes on remembering deep in his being that he has lost a paradise.

It is not a coincidence that all the religions of the world have the idea in parables that once man lived in paradise and somehow, for some reason he has been expelled from that paradise. They are different stories, different parables, but signifying one simple truth: these stories are just a poetic way to say that every man is born in paradise and then loses it. The retarded, the unintelligent completely forget about it.

But the intelligent, the sensitive, the creative go on being haunted by the paradise that they have known once and now only a faint memory, unbelievable, has remained with them. They start searching for it again.

The search for paradise is the search for your childhood again. Of course your body will no more be a child's, but your consciousness can be as pure as the consciousness of the child. This is the whole secret of the mystical path: to make you a child again, innocent, unpolluted by any knowledge, not knowing anything, still aware of everything that surrounds you, with a deep wonder and a sense of a mystery that cannot be demystified.

PLAYFULNESS

Nobody allows their children to dance and to sing and to shout and to jump. For trivial reasons—perhaps something may get broken, perhaps they may get their clothes wet in the rain if they run out; for these small things—a great spiritual quality, playfulness, is completely destroyed.

The obedient child is praised by his parents, by his teachers, by everybody, and the playful child is condemned. His playfulness may be absolutely harmless, but he is condemned because there is potentially a danger of rebellion. If the child goes on growing with full freedom to be playful, he will turn out to be a rebel. He will not be easily enslaved; he will not be easily put into armies to destroy people or to be destroyed himself.

The rebellious child will turn out to be a rebellious youth. Then you cannot force marriage on him; then you cannot force him into a particular job; then the child cannot be forced to fulfill the unfulfilled desires and longings of the parents. The rebellious youth will go his own way. He will live his life according to his own innermost desires, not according to somebody else's ideals.

For all these reasons playfulness is stifled, crushed from the very beginning. Your nature is never allowed to have its say. Slowly, slowly you start carrying a dead child within yourself. This dead child within you destroys your sense of humor: you cannot laugh with your total heart, you cannot play, you cannot enjoy the small things of life. You become so serious that your life, rather then expanding, starts shrinking.

Life should be, each moment, a precious creativity. What you create does not matter—it may be just sand castles on the seashore, but whatever you do should come out of your playfulness and joy.

INTELLIGENCE

Intelligence is not something that is acquired; it is inbuilt, it is inborn, it is intrinsic to life itself. Not only children are intelligent, animals are intelligent in their own way, trees are intelligent in their own way. Of course they all have different kinds of intelligences because their needs differ, but now it is an established fact that all that lives is intelligent. Life cannot be without intelligence; to be alive and to be intelligent are synonymous. But man is in a dilemma for the simple reason that he is not only intelligent, he is also aware of his intelligence. That is something unique about man— his privilege, his prerogative, his glory—but it can turn very easily into his agony. Man is conscious that he is intelligent, and that consciousness brings its own problems. The first problem is that it creates ego.

Ego does not exist anywhere else except in human beings, and ego starts growing as the child grows. The parents, the schools, colleges, universities, they all help to strengthen the ego for the simple reason that for centuries man had to struggle to survive and the idea has become a fixation, a deep unconscious conditioning that only strong egos can survive in the struggle of life. Life has become just a struggle to survive. And scientists have made it even more convincing with the theory of the survival of the fittest. So we help every child to become more and more strong in the ego, and it is there that the problem arises.

As the ego becomes strong it starts surrounding intelligence like a thick layer of darkness. Intelligence is light, ego is darkness. Intelligence is very delicate, ego is very hard. Intelligence is like a rose flower, ego is like a rock. And if you want to survive, they say—the so-called knowers—then you have to become rocklike, you have to be strong, invulnerable. You have to become a citadel, a closed citadel, so you cannot be attacked from outside. You have to become impenetrable.

But then you become closed. Then you start dying as far as your intelligence is concerned because intelligence needs the open sky, the wind, the air, the sun in order to grow, to expand, to flow. To remain alive it needs a constant flow; if it becomes stagnant it slowly becomes a dead phenomenon.

We don't allow children to remain intelligent. The first thing is that if they are intelligent they will be vulnerable, they will be delicate, they will be open. If they are intelligent they will be able to see many falsities in the society, in the state, in the church, in the educational system. They will become rebellious. They will be individuals; they will not be cowed easily. You can crush them, but you cannot enslave them. You can destroy them, but you cannot force them to compromise.

In one sense intelligence is very soft, like a rose flower, in another sense it has its own strength. But that strength is subtle, not gross. That strength is the strength of rebellion, of a noncompromising attitude. One is not ready to sell one's soul.

Watch small children and then you will see their intelligence. Yes, they are not knowledgeable—if you want them to be knowledgeable, then you will not think that they are intelligent. If you ask them questions that depend on information, then they will look not intelligent. But ask them real questions, which have nothing to do with information, which need an immediate response, and see—they are far more intelligent than you are. Of course your ego won't allow you to accept it, but if you can accept it, it will help tremendously. It will help you, it will help your children, because if you can see their intelligence you can learn much from them.

Even though the society destroys your intelligence it cannot destroy it totally; it only covers it with many layers of information.

And that's the whole function of meditation: to take you deeper into yourself. It is a method of digging into your own being to the point when you come to the living waters of your own intelligence, when you discover the springs of your own intelligence. When you have discovered your child again, only then will you understand what I mean by emphasizing again and again that children are really intelligent.

The mother was preparing little Pedro to go to a party. When she finished combing his hair she straightened his shirt collar and said, "Go now, son. Have a good time . . . and behave yourself!"

"Come on, mother!" said Pedro. "Please decide before I leave which it is going to be!"

You see the point? The mother was saying, "Have a good time . . . and behave yourself." Now, both things cannot be done together. And the child's response is really of tremendous value. He says, "Please decide before I leave which it is going to be. If you allow me to have a good time, then I cannot behave; if you want me to behave, then I cannot have a good time." The child can see the contradiction so clearly; it may not have been apparent to the mother.

A passerby asks a boy, "Son, can you please tell me what time it is?"

"Yes, of course," replies the boy, "but what do you need it for? It changes continuously!"

A new transit sign was put in front of the school. It read: Drive Slowly. Do Not Kill a Student!

The following day there was another sign under it scribbled in a childish writing: Wait for the Teacher!

Little Pierino comes home from school with a big smile on his face.

"Well, dear, you look very happy. So you like school, do you?"

"Don't be silly, Mom," replies the boy. "We must not confuse the going with the coming back!"

While slowly walking to school the little boy prays, "Dear God, please do not let me arrive at school late. I pray you, God, let me arrive at school on time . . ."

At this moment he slips on a banana peel and slides down the path for a few meters. Pulling himself up he looks at the sky annoyed and says, "Okay, okay, God, there is no need to push!"

The young teacher wrote on the blackboard, "I ain't had no fun all summer." Then she asked the children, "What is wrong with that sentence and what do I do to correct it?"

Little Ernie shouted from the back, "Get a boyfriend."

The father was telling stories to his sons in the living room after dinner. "My great-grandfather fought in the war against the dictator Rosas, my uncle fought in the war against the Kaiser, my grandfather fought in the war of Spain against the Republicans and my father fought in the Second World War against the Germans."

To which the smallest son replied, "What's wrong with this family? They can't relate to anybody!"

INNOCENCE

Small children are innocent but they have not earned it; it is natural. They are ignorant really, but their ignorance is better than the so-called learning because the learned person is simply covering his ignorance with words, theories, ideologies, philosophies, dogmas, creeds. He is trying to cover up his ignorance, but just scratch him a little bit and you will find inside nothing but darkness, nothing but ignorance.

A child is in a far better state than the learned person because they can see things. Even though they are ignorant they are spontaneous, even though they are ignorant they have insights of tremendous value.

A little boy, seized with hiccups, cried, "Mommy, I am coughing backwards!"

A small boy was brought to a psychiatrist's office for an examination by the mother who was a chatterbox. The psychiatrist examined the little fellow and was surprised that he hardly paid any attention to the questions.

"Do you have trouble hearing?" the psychiatrist asked him.

"No," replied the lad. "I have trouble listening."

You see the insight? Hearing and listening are tremendously different. The child was saying, "I have no difficulty in hearing, but I am tired of listening. One has to hear—the chatterbox mother is there—but I have trouble listening. I cannot pay attention." The mother being a chatterbox has destroyed something valuable in the child: his attentiveness. He is utterly bored.

The second-grade teacher had sent the children to the board to work out arithmetic problems. One little fellow said, "I ain't got no chalk."

"That's not right," the teacher said. "The right way to say it is, 'I don't have any chalk. You don't have any chalk, we don't have any chalk, they don't have any chalk . . .' Now do you understand?"

"No," said the little boy. "What happened to all the chalk?"

The clock had just struck 3 a.m. when the minister's teenage daughter returned from a dance. The minister and his wife had been waiting up for the girl, and as she came in the front door he said to her rather scornfully, "Good morning, child of the devil."

Speaking sweetly, as any child should, she said, "Good morning, Father."

The teacher was trying to teach subtraction. "Now, Hugh," she said, "if your father earned $180 a week and if they deducted $6 for insurance, $10.80 for social security, and $24 for taxes, and then if he gave your mother half, what would she have?"

"A heart attack!" the kid said.

Supper was over. The father of the house and his nine-year-old son were in the living room watching television. Mother and daughter were in the kitchen, washing up the supper dishes. Suddenly the father and son heard a terrible crashing sound of something being broken in the kitchen. They waited for a moment in shock but did not hear a sound.

"It was Mom who broke the dish," said the boy.

"How do you know?" his father asked.

"Because," replied his son, "she's not saying anything!"

From the kitchen came the sound of the crash of either broken glass or broken china.

"Willy," cried his mother from the living room. "What on earth are you doing in the kitchen?"

"Nothing," Willy said, "it's already done!"

A salesman who had been working in the New England area was being transferred to California. The move had been the principal topic of conversation around the house for weeks.

Then the night before the big move, when his five-year-old daughter was saying her prayers, she said, "And now, God, I will have to say good-bye forever because tomorrow we are moving to California!"

How did you manage to stay with your innocence and clarity as a child and not let yourself become intimidated by the grown-ups around you? Where did you get that courage from?

Innocence is courage and clarity both. There is no need to have courage if you are innocent. There is no need, either, for any clarity because nothing can be more crystal clear than innocence. So the whole question is how to protect one's own innocence. Innocence is not something to be achieved. It is not something to be learned. It is not something like a talent for painting, music, poetry, sculpture. It is not like those things. It is more like breathing, something you are born with. Innocence is everybody's nature.

Nobody is born other than innocent. How can one be born other than innocent? Birth means you have entered the world as a tabula rasa, nothing is written on you. You have only future, no past. That is the meaning of innocence. So first try to understand all the meanings of innocence.

The first is: no past, only future. You come as an innocent watcher into the world. Everybody comes in the same way, with the same quality of consciousness.

The question is, how did I manage so that nobody could corrupt my innocence, clarity; from where did I get this courage? How could I manage not to be humiliated by grown-ups and their world? I have not done anything, so there is no question of how. It simply happened, so I cannot take the credit for it. Perhaps it happens to everybody but you become interested in other things. You start bargaining with the grown-up world. They have many things to give to you; you have only one thing to give, and that is your integrity, your self-respect. You don't have much, a single thing— you can call it anything: innocence, intelligence, authenticity. You have only one thing.

And the child is naturally very much interested in everything he sees around. He is continuously wanting to have this, to have that; that is part of human nature. If you look at the small child, even a just-born baby, you can see he has started groping for something; his hands are trying to find out something. He has started the journey.

In the journey he will lose himself, because you can't get anything in this world without paying for it. And the poor child cannot understand that what he is giving is so valuable that if the whole world is on one side and his integrity is on the other side, then too his integrity will be more weighty, more valuable. The child has no way to know about it. This is the problem—because what he has, he simply has; he takes it for granted.

You are asking me how I managed not to lose my innocence and clarity. I have not done anything; just simply, from the very beginning . . . I was a lonely child because I was brought up by my maternal grandfather and grandmother; I was not with my father and mother. Those two old people were alone and they wanted a child who would be the joy of their last days. So my father and mother agreed: I was their eldest child, the firstborn, and they sent me to live with my grandparents.

I don't remember any relationship with my father's family in the early years of my childhood. I lived with these two old men—my grandfather and his old servant, who was really a beautiful man — and my old grandmother . . . three people. And the gap was so great, I was absolutely alone. They were not company for me, could not be company. They tried their hardest to be as friendly to me as possible but it was just not possible.

I was left to myself. I could not say things to them. I had nobody else, because in that small village my family was the richest. And it was such a small village—not more than two hundred people in all—and so poor that my grandparents would not allow me to mix with the village children. They were dirty, and of course they were almost beggars. So there was no way to have friends. That caused a great impact. In my whole life I have never been a friend and I have never known anybody to be a friend. Yes, acquaintances I had.

In those first, early years I was so lonely that I started enjoying it; and it is really a joy. So it was not a curse to me, it proved a blessing. I started enjoying it and I started feeling self-sufficient; I was not dependent on anybody.

I have never been interested in games for the simple reason that from my very childhood there was no way to play, there was no-body to play with. I can still see myself in those earliest years, just sitting.

We had a beautiful spot where our house was, just in front of a lake. Far away for miles, the lake stretched . . . and it was so beautiful and so silent. Only once in a while would you see a line of white cranes flying, or hear them making love calls, and the peace would be disturbed; otherwise, it was exactly the right place for meditation. And when they would disturb the peace . . . a love call from a bird, and after his call the peace would deepen, it would become deeper.

The lake was full of lotus flowers, and I would sit for hours so self-content, as if the world did not matter: the lotuses, the white cranes, the silence. . . . And my grandparents became very aware of one thing, that I enjoyed my aloneness. They had seen that I never had any desire to go to the village to meet anybody, or to talk with anybody. Even if they wanted to talk to me, my answers were yes or no; I was not interested in talking either. So they became aware of one thing, that I enjoyed my aloneness, and it was their sacred duty not to disturb me.

It happens with children that you tell them, "Be silent because your father is thinking, your grandfather is resting. Be quiet, sit silently." In my childhood it happened the opposite way. Now I cannot answer why and how; it simply happened. That's why I said it simply happened—the credit does not go to me.

All those three old people were continually making signs to each other: "Don't disturb him, he is enjoying so much." And they started loving my silence.

Silence has its vibe; it is infectious, particularly a child's silence which is not forced, which is not because you are saying, "I will beat you if you create any nuisance or noise." No, that is not silence. That will not create the joyous vibration that I am talking about, when a child is silent on his own, enjoying for no reason, his happiness is uncaused; that creates great ripples all around.

In a better world, every family will learn from children. You are in such a hurry to teach them. Nobody seems to learn from them, and they have much to teach you. And you have nothing to teach them.

Just because you are older and powerful you start making them just like you without ever thinking about what you are, where you have reached, what your status is in the inner world. You are a pauper, and you want the same for your child also? But nobody thinks; otherwise people would learn from small children. Children bring so much from the other world because they are such fresh arrivals. They still carry the silence of the womb, the silence of the very existence.

So it was just a coincidence that for seven years I remained undisturbed with no one to nag me, to prepare me for the world of business, politics, diplomacy. My grandparents were more interested in leaving me as natural as possible—particularly my grandmother. She is one of the causes—these small things affect all your life patterns—she is one of the causes of my respect for the whole of womanhood. She was a simple woman, uneducated, but immensely sensitive. She made it clear to my grandfather and the servant: "We all have lived a certain kind of life which has not led us anywhere. We are as empty as ever, and now death is coming close." She insisted, "Let this child be uninfluenced by us. What influence can we contribute? We can only make him like us, and we are nothing. Give him an opportunity to be himself."

I am tremendously grateful to that old woman. My grandfather was again and again worried that sooner or later he was going to be responsible: "They will say, 'We left our child with you and you have not taught him anything.'"

My grandmother did not even allow me to be educated. Because there was one man in the village who could at least teach me the beginnings of language, mathematics, a little geography. He was educated to the fourth grade—the lowest four of what was called primary education in India. But he was the most educated man in the town. My grandfather tried hard: "He can come and he can teach him. At least he will know the alphabet, some mathematics, so when he goes to his parents they will not say that we just wasted seven years completely."

But my grandmother said, "Let them do whatsoever they want to do after seven years. For seven years he has to be just his natural self, and we are not going to interfere." And her argument was always, "You know the alphabet, so what? You know mathematics, so what? You have earned a little money; do you want him also to earn a little money and live just like you?"

That was enough to keep that old man silent. What to do? He was in a difficulty because he could not argue, but he knew that he would be held responsible, not she, because my father would ask him, "What have you done?" And actually that would have been the case, but fortunately he died before my father could ask.

When I went back to my parents, my father continually was saying, "That old man is responsible, he has spoiled the child." But now I was strong enough, and I made it clear to him: "Before me, never say a single word against my maternal grandfather. He has saved me from being spoiled by you—that is your real anger. But you have other children—spoil them. And at the final stage you will see who is spoiled."

He had other children, and more and more children went on coming. I used to tease him, "You please bring one child more, make it a dozen." Eleven children? People ask, 'How many children?' Eleven does not look right; one dozen is more impressive."

And in later years I used to tell him, "You go on spoiling all your children; I am wild, and I will remain wild."

What you see as innocence is nothing but wildness. What you

see as clarity is nothing but wildness. Somehow I remained out of the grip of civilization.

Once I was strong enough . . . and that's why people insist, "Take hold of the child as quickly as possible, don't waste time because the earlier you take hold of the child, the easier it is. Once the child becomes strong enough, then to bend him according to your desires will be difficult."

And life moves in seven-year circles. By the seventh year the child is perfectly strong; now you cannot do anything. Now he knows where to go, what to do. He is capable of arguing. He is capable of seeing what is right and what is wrong. And his clarity will be at the climax when he is seven. If you don't disturb his earlier years, then at the seventh he is so crystal clear about everything that his whole life will be lived without any repentance.

I have lived without any repentance. I have tried to find: Have I done anything wrong, ever? Not that people have been thinking that all that I have done is right, that is not the point: *I* have never thought anything that I have done was wrong. The whole world may think it was wrong, but to me there is absolute certainty that it was right; it was the right thing to do.

2

pregnancy, childbirth, infancy

If enlightened beings don't have children, and neurotic people are unfit for parenthood, when is the right time?

Enlightened persons don't have children; neurotic persons should not have. Just between the two, there is a state of mental health, of non-neurosis: you are neither neurotic nor enlightened, simply healthy. Just in the middle—that is the right time for parenthood, to become a mother or to become a father.

This is the trouble: neurotic persons tend to have many children. Neurotic persons tend, in their neurosis, to create a very occupied space around them. They should not, because that is avoiding. They should face the fact of neurosis and they should go beyond it.

An enlightened person need not have children. He has given the ultimate birth to himself. Now there is no need to give birth to anything else. He has become a father and mother to himself. He has become a womb to himself, and he is reborn.

But between the two, when the neurosis is not there, you medi-

tate, you become a little alert, aware. Your life is not just of darkness. The light is not as penetrating as it is when one becomes a
buddha, but a dim candlelight is available. That is the right time to
have children, because then you will be able to give something of
your awareness to your children. Otherwise, what will you give as a
gift to them? You will give your neurosis.

I have heard: A man with eighteen children took them to a
dairy cattle show. Included in the show was a prize bull and
there was a charge of fifty cents to go in and see it. The man
thought that this charge was exorbitant, but his children
wanted to see the animal, and so they approached the entrance
to its enclosure. The attendant said, "Are all these children
yours, sir?"

"Yes, they are," answered the man. "Why?"

The attendant replied, "Well, wait here a minute and I
will bring the bull out to see you!"

Eighteen children! Even the bull will feel jealous.

You go on unconsciously reproducing replicas of yourself. First
think: Are you in such a state that if you give birth to a child, you
will be giving a gift to the world? Are you a blessing to the world, or
a curse? And then think: Are you ready to mother or to father a
child? Are you ready to give love unconditionally? Because children
come through you, but they don't belong to you. You can give your
love to them, but you should not impose your ideas on them. You
should not give your neurotic ways of living to them. Will you allow them to flower in their own way? Will you allow them freedom
to be themselves? If you are ready, then it is okay. Otherwise, wait;
become ready.

With man, conscious evolution has entered into the world.
Don't be like animals, just reproducing unconsciously. Now get

ready before you decide to have a child. Become more meditative, become more quiet and peaceful. Get rid of all the neurosis that you have within you. Wait for that moment when you are absolutely clean, then give birth to a child. Then give your life to the child, your love to the child. You will be helping to create a better world.

I am pregnant. I had decided to have an abortion and thought I was happy with the decision, but since then, whenever I think about it I feel sad.

This will be a momentary sadness. If you want to become a mother then you want to get into deeper troubles, because it is not a question that can be easily solved once the child is there. The mother cannot have her own growth, she cannot work; she has to take care of the children. And then there are complications.

Once you have finished your own growth work then it is perfectly good. A child should be a leisure thing, it should be the last luxury. Then you can treat yourself by being a mother, otherwise it will create complications. So you decide. Nobody is forcing you, it is for you to decide: if you want to become a mother then you want to become a mother. But then take the consequences also.

People are not aware of what they are doing when they want to bring a child into the world. Otherwise they will feel sorry about that, rather than feeling sorry about an abortion. Just think of both the possibilities: What will you give to the child? What have you got to give to the child?

You will bring your tensions into his being and he will repeat the same kind of life as yours. He will go to the psychoanalyst, he will go to the psychiatrist, and his whole life will be a problem— just as it is with everybody. What right have you to bring a soul into the world when you cannot give the person a whole and healthy being? It is a crime! People think otherwise: they think abortion is a crime. But the child will find some other mother, because nothing dies. And there are many, many women who will be happy to have the child; it is just that you will not be responsible for it.

I am not saying not to become a mother; I am saying be aware that becoming a mother is a great art, it is a great achievement. First create that quality, that creativity in you, that joy, that celebration, and then invite the child. Then you will have something to give to the child—your celebration, your song, your dance—and you will not create a pathological being. The world is already too crowded with pathological beings. Let some other planet suffer! Why this earth? The world is starving, food is not there and people are dying, the whole ecology is disturbed and life is going to be more and more ugly and hellish; this is not the right time.

And even if you think that it is okay, that the world will look after itself, they will find some way, you still have to think about your child. Are you ready to be a mother? That is the thing. If you think you are ready, go ahead: have a child. When you are prepared you will be happy to have a child and the child will be happy that he was fortunate to have a mother like you. Otherwise just go to any psychiatrist and ask, "What are people's problems?" They can be reduced to one thing: the mother, because the mother was not capable of giving a psychological womb, the mother was not capable of giving a spiritual womb. Psychologically she was neurotic, spiritually she was empty, so there was no spiritual food for the child, no nourishment. The child comes into the world as a physical being, without a soul, without any center. The mother was not centered; how can the child be centered? The child is simply a continuation, a continuity of the mother's being. If one sees all the implications of it, fewer people will decide to become fathers and mothers. And it would be a better world if fewer people decided to be mothers and fathers. It would be less crowded, less neurotic, less pathological, less crazy.

We don't have any children yet and I have some feeling to have a child. I'm thirty-two now and I feel ready, but I would like your advice.

Just one thing. Whenever you make love, always make love after meditation. Make it a point that you meditate, and when the energy is very meditative, only then make love. When you are in a deep meditative state and the energy is flowing, you conceive a higher quality soul. What type of soul enters you depends on where you are.

It almost always happens that people make love when they are sexual. Sexuality is a lower center. It happens sometimes that when people are angry and fighting, they make love. That too is very low. You open your door to a much lower soul. Or people make love as a routine, a mechanical habit, something that has to be done every day, or twice a week, or whatever. They do it just as a mechanical routine or as part of physical hygiene, but then it is very mechanical. It has nothing of your heart in it, and then you allow very low souls to enter you.

Love should be almost like prayer. Love is sacred. It is the holiest thing that exists in man.

So first one should prepare oneself to move into love. Pray, meditate, and when you are full of a different kind of energy that has nothing to do with the physical, in fact nothing to do with the sexual, then you are vulnerable to a higher quality soul. So much depends on the mother.

If you are not very alert about it, you will get entangled with a very ordinary soul. People are almost unaware of what they are doing. If you go to purchase a car, even then you think much about it. If you go to purchase furniture for your room, you have a thousand and one alternatives and you think about this and that, which one will suit. But as far as children are concerned, you never think about what type of children you would like, what type of soul you are going to invoke, invite.

And millions are the alternatives . . . from Judas to Jesus, from the darkest soul to the holiest. Millions are the alternatives and your attitude will decide. Whatsoever your attitude, you become available to that sort of soul.

I'm pregnant. Is there any meditation or anything to do that will be helpful for the baby or for us as the parents?

Just remain as happy and loving as possible. Avoid negativities—that's what destroys the mind of the child. When the child is in formation he not only follows your body, he follows your mind too, because those are the blueprints. So if you are negative, that negativity starts entering into the makeup of the child from the very beginning. Then it is a long, arduous journey to drop it. If mothers were a little more careful, no primal scream therapy would be needed. If mothers were a little more careful, psychoanalysis as a profession would disappear.

Psychoanalysis is doing great business because of mothers. The mother is really of great significance because for nine months the child will live in the climate of the mother; he will imbibe her mind, her whole mind. So don't be negative. Be more and more in the yes mood—even sometimes when it looks hard. But that much sacrifice has to be made for the child. If you really want to have a child of some value, of some integrity, of some individuality, and a happy child, then that sacrifice has to be made. That is part of being a mother—that sacrifice. So don't be negative at all; avoid all negativities. Avoid anger, avoid jealousy, avoid possessiveness, nagging, fighting; avoid these spaces. These you cannot afford—you are creating a new being! The work is of such importance that one cannot be silly and stupid.

Rejoice more and more, pray, dance, sing, listen to great music—not pop music. Listen to classical music, which is soothing and goes very deep into the unconscious, because the child can hear it only from there.

Sit silently as much as you can, enjoy nature. Be with trees, birds, animals, because they are really innocent. They are still part of the Garden of Eden—only Adam and Eve have been thrown out. Even the tree of knowledge is still in the Garden of Eden; only Adam and Eve have been thrown out. So be with nature more, and relax so that the child grows in a relaxed womb, non-tense; otherwise from the very beginning the child starts becoming neurotic.

(To the father): And help her in these days so that she can be more positive. Don't provoke her into negativity. Give her more and more time so that she can sit silently, be with the trees, listen to the birds, the music. Avoid any situation in which you think it can become a provocation for her to become negative. Be more loving, rejoice in each other's silence more, because you are both giving birth to something that is divine. Each child is divine, and when something great is going to happen, a great guest is going to come to your home, you don't fight. And this may be the greatest guest that will ever come to you, so for these nine months be careful, cautious, watchful.

Be more loving and less sexual. If sex happens out of being loving, it's okay, but not for sex's sake itself. From the very beginning that gives the child a deep-rooted sexuality. Sex is perfectly good in the context of love, as part of love—just as you hold hands and hug each other as a part of love. One day you make love too, but as part of love. It is not sexuality then; it is just a communion.

If for these nine months you can avoid sex as sex, that will be a great gift to the child. Then his life will not be so obsessed with sex as people's lives are.

Is there something that the mother can do to make the process of birth as easy as possible for the child?

Certainly the mother can do much, but you can do only by nondoing. So simply relax. Noninterference has to be remembered, and when you start feeling the pain simply go with the pain. When you start feeling the movements in the womb, and the body starts getting ready to give birth, and there is a rhythmic pulse inside . . . That pulse people think is painful; it is not painful, it is our wrong interpretation that makes it painful. So when the pulse arises, simply accept it, float with it. It is just like breathing in, breathing out, so the womb and the birth channel start expanding, shrinking. That is just a way to make a passage for the child. When you feel it is pain, when you decide it is pain, you start fighting with it because it is very difficult not to fight with pain. When you start fighting you start an interference with the rhythm. That interference is very destructive to the child. If the mother simply helps the child, if the mother goes with the body, whatsoever is happening—expands with the body, shrinks with the body, allows the pulse and simply enjoys it—it is really a great delight. But it depends how you take it.

For example, now at least in the West people have more advanced ideas about sex. Otherwise in the past all down the centuries the first sexual experience for the woman was very painful. She was just trembling because from the very childhood it was taught that it is very ugly, animalistic, so she was just shaking with fear. The honeymoon would come close and the woman would be trembling. She feels that she has to go through the ordeal—it was an ordeal, and of course then it was painful. But now in the West at least, the pain has disappeared. It is a beautiful experience, it is orgasmic.

It is exactly the same thing with childbirth. It is greater orgasm than sexual orgasm, because in a sexual orgasm your body takes a

rhythm: expands, shrinks, expands, shrinks, but it is nothing com-
pared to when you are giving birth to a child. To give birth to a
child is a million-fold bigger orgasm. If you take it as an orgasm—
happy, delighted, rejoicing in it, that's all—then the child simply
comes out of the passage, helped by you. Otherwise if the mother is
fighting—the child wants to come out and the mother is fighting,
and she is not allowing the movement that is needed for it, the necessary movement—sometimes the child gets stuck, the head gets
stuck. If the head is stuck, the child will suffer his whole life. He
will not be as intelligent as he would have been, because his head is
very soft and the brain is still developing. Just a little shock, just a
little closing, and the brain is no longer as healthy as it could have
been.

So help it, enjoy it. Just take it as if you are moving in a great
orgasm, nothing else. No interference on your part is the greatest
help for a child. Then the child comes easily, relaxed, in a let-go.
And then your child will not need Primal therapy, otherwise each
person needs Primal therapy because everybody has suffered a birth
trauma. And it has been so painful for the child. It is just the first
experience, and the first experience is so ugly, suffocating, almost
killing the child: the passage is narrow and the mother is tense and
the child cannot come out of the passage.

This is his first experience. So the first experience is of hell, and
then the whole life becomes miserable. Let the first experience be of
a beautiful flowing, and that will be the foundation for the child.

**What else can be done so that the birth of a child is made as
gentle as possible?**

When the child comes out of the womb, it is the greatest shock
of his life. Even death will not be this big a shock, because death
will come without warning. Death will come most probably when
he is unconscious. But while he is coming out of the mother's

womb, he is conscious. His nine months' long sleep, peaceful sleep, is disturbed—and then you cut the thread that joins him with the mother. The moment you cut that thread that joins him with the mother, you have created a fearful individual. This is not the right way; but this is how it has been done up to now.

The child should be taken away from the mother more slowly, more gradually. There should not be that shock—and it can be arranged. A scientific arrangement is possible. There should not be glaring lights in the room, because the child has lived for nine months in absolute darkness, and he has very fragile eyes that have never seen light. And in all your hospitals there are glaring lights, tube lights, and the child suddenly faces the light . . . Most people are suffering from weak eyes because of this; later on they have to use glasses. No animal needs them. Have you seen animals with glasses reading the newspaper? Their eyes are perfectly healthy their whole life, to the point of death. It is only man. And the beginning is at the *very* beginning. No, the child should be given birth in darkness, or in a very soft light, candles perhaps. Darkness would be the best, but if a little light is needed, then candles will do.

And what have the doctors been doing up to now? They don't even give a little time for the child to be acquainted with the new reality. The way they welcome the child has been so ugly. They would hang the child with his feet in their hands and slap his bottom. The idea behind this stupid ritual is that this will help the child to breathe—because in the mother's womb he was not breathing on his own; the mother was breathing for him, eating for him, doing everything for him.

To be welcomed into the world hanging upside down, with a slap on your bottom, is not a very good beginning. But the doctor is in a hurry. Otherwise the child would start breathing on his own; he has to be left on the mother's belly, on top of the mother's belly. Before the joining thread is cut, he should be left on the mother's belly. He was inside the belly, beneath; now he is outside. That is not a great change. The mother is there, he can touch her, he can feel her. He knows the vibe. He is perfectly aware that this is his home. He has come out, but this is his home. Let him be with the mother a little longer, so he becomes acquainted with the mother from the outside; from the inside he knows her.

And don't cut the thread that joins him till he starts breathing on his own. Right now, what is done? We cut the thread and slap the child so he has to breathe. But this is forcing him, this is violent, and absolutely unscientific and unnatural. Let him first breathe on his own. It will take a few minutes. Don't be in such a hurry. It is a question of a man's whole life. You can smoke your cigarette two or three minutes later, you can whisper sweet nothings to your girlfriend a few minutes later. It is not going to harm anybody. What is the rush? You can't give him three minutes? A child needs no more than that. Just left on his own, within three minutes he starts breathing. When he starts breathing, he becomes confident that he can live on his own. Then you can cut the thread, it is useless now; it will not give a shock to the child.

Then the most significant thing is, don't put him in blankets and in a bed. No, for nine months he was without blankets, naked, without pillows, without bedsheets, without a bed—don't make such a change so quickly. He needs a small tub with the same solution of water that was in his mother's womb—it is just like ocean water: the same amount of salt, the same amount of chemicals, exactly the same.

That is again a proof that life must have happened first in the ocean. It still happens in the oceanic water.

That's why when a woman is pregnant she starts eating salty things, because the womb goes on absorbing the salt—the child needs exactly the same salty water that exists in the ocean. So just make up the same water in a small tub, and let the child lie down in the tub, and he will feel perfectly welcomed. This is the situation he is acquainted with.

In Japan, one Zen monk has tried a tremendous experiment, and that is helping a three-month-old child to swim. Slowly he has been coming down in age. First he tried with nine-month-old children, then with six-month-old children, now with three-month-old children. And I say to him that you are still far away. Even the child just born is capable of swimming, because he has been swimming in his mother's womb.

So give the child a chance, similar to the mother's womb.

FEEDING AND LOVING THE CHILD

When a mother is feeding her child, she is not only giving milk as was always thought. Now biologists have stumbled upon a deeper fact, and they say she is feeding energy—milk is just the physical part. And they have done many experiments: a child is raised, food is given—as perfect as possible, whatsoever medical science has found is needed. Everything is given, but the child is not loved, not cuddled; the mother does not touch him. The milk is given through mechanical devices, injections are given, vitamins are given—everything is perfect. But the child stops growing, he starts shrinking, as if life starts moving away from him. What is happening? Whatsoever the mother's milk was giving is being given, but the child does not thrive.

It happened in Germany that during the war many small orphan babies were put into a hospital. Within weeks they were all almost dying. Half of them died—and every care was taken; scientifically they were absolutely right, they were doing whatsoever was needed. But why were these children dying? Then one psychoanalyst observed that they needed some cuddling, somebody to hug them, somebody to make them feel significant. Food is not food enough. Some inner food, some invisible food is needed. So the psychoanalyst made a rule that whosoever came into the room—a nurse, a doctor, a servant—had to spend at least five minutes in the room hugging and playing with the children. Suddenly they were not dying, they started growing. And since then many studies have been done.

When a mother hugs a child, energy is flowing. That energy is invisible—we have called it love, warmth. Something is jumping from the mother to the child, and not only from the mother to the child, from the child to the mother also. That's why a woman is never so beautiful as when she becomes a mother. Before, something is lacking, she is not complete, the circle is broken. Whenever a woman becomes a mother, the circle is complete. A grace comes to her as if from some unknown source. So not only is she feeding the child, the child is also feeding the mother. They are happily "into" each other.

And there is no other relationship which is so close. Even lovers are not so close, because the child comes from the mother, from her very blood, her flesh and bones; the child is just an extension of her being. Never again will this happen, because nobody can be so close. A lover can be near your heart, but the child has lived inside the heart. For nine months he remained as part of the mother, organically joined, one. The mother's life was his life, the mother's death would have been his death. Even afterward it goes on: a transfer of energy, a communication of energy exists.

· · ·

The mother becomes from the very beginning associated with the idea of food and love. They become almost like two aspects of the same coin. The child's love object and his food object are the same. Not only the mother but the breast in particular: he gets the food from the breast and the warmth and the feel of love.

There is a difference: when the mother loves the child, the breast has a different feel and different vibe. The mother enjoys the child feeding on her breast; it is stimulating to the mother's sexuality. If the mother is really in love with the child she goes almost into an orgasmic joy. Her breasts are very sensitive; they are the most erotic zones of her body. She starts glowing and the child can feel it. The child becomes aware of the phenomenon that the mother is enjoying. She is not simply feeding him, she is enjoying it.

But when the mother gives the breast just out of necessity, then the breast is cold; there is no warmth in it. The mother is unwilling, she is in a hurry. She wants to snatch the breast away as quickly as possible. And the child feels that. It is so apparent that the mother is cold, she is unloving, she is not warm. She is not really a mother. The child seems to be unwanted, feels unwanted.

The child feels wanted only when the mother enjoys the child feeding on the breast, when it becomes almost a loving relationship, almost an orgasmic relationship. Only then the child feels love from the mother, needed by the mother. And to be needed by the mother is to be needed by existence because the mother is his whole existence; he knows the existence through the mother. Whatsoever is his idea about the mother is going to be his idea of the world.

A child who has not been loved by the mother will find himself alienated in existence; he will find himself an outsider, a stranger. He cannot trust in existence. He could not even trust in his own mother, how can he trust in anybody else? Trust becomes impossible. He doubts, he is suspicious; he is continuously on guard, afraid, scared. He finds everywhere enemies, competitors. He is every moment afraid of being crushed and destroyed. The world does not seem to him to be a home at all.

If the mother is happy, rejoices in feeding the child, then the child never eats too much because he trusts; he knows the mother is always there. Any time he is hungry his needs will be fulfilled. He never eats too much.

A well-loved child remains healthy. He is neither thin nor fat; he keeps a balance.

. . .

Just look at a small child. Whenever he feels tense he will put his hand in his mouth, he will start chewing his own hand. And why does he feel good when his thumb is in his mouth? Why does the child feel good and go to sleep? This is the way of almost all children. Whenever they feel sleep is not coming they will put the thumb inside the mouth, feel at ease, and fall asleep. Why? The thumb becomes a substitute for the mother's breast, and food is relaxing. You cannot go to sleep on a hungry stomach, it is difficult to get to sleep. When the stomach is full you feel sleepy, the body needs rest. The thumb is just a substitute for the breast; it is not giving milk, it is a false thing, but still it gives the feeling.

When this child grows, if he sucks his thumb in public you will think he is foolish, so he takes a cigarette. A cigarette is not foolish, it is accepted. It is just the thumb, and more harmful than the thumb. It is better if you smoke your thumb, go on smoking to your grave; it is not harmful, it is better.

And in countries where breast-feeding has stopped, more smoking will automatically be there. That's why people in the developed countries smoke more than people in underdeveloped countries—no mother is ready to give her breast to the child because the shape is lost. In all primitive communities a seven-year-old child, or even an eight- or nine-year-old child, will continue breast-feeding. Then there is a satisfaction and smoking will not be so necessary. And that's why in primitive communities men are not so much interested in women's breasts; nobody looks at the breasts.

If you had been given the breast for ten years continuously, you would get fed up and bored, you would say, "Stop now!" But every child has been taken away from the breast prematurely, and that remains a wound. So all civilized countries are obsessed with breasts. Children should be given the breast; otherwise they will become addicted to it, the whole life they will be in search of it.

. . .

Scientists have experimented with young children to see what they will do if they are left near food. You will think they would overeat. You are wrong, they don't overeat. Their mother and father overfeed them saying, "Eat more. Eat, get a little more robust. Show a little radiance, look at you! Eat a little more." The mother is sitting on your chest saying eat more, just a little more. The child is crying and somehow managing to eat. You often see children crying. His body is saying no. His body is saying go outside, jump and leap a little, go climb trees. And you go on feeding him. The doctor says that every three hours the child needs to be given milk. The child is not drinking, and he turns his face this way and that. But the mother goes on feeding him milk because three hours have passed. This following the average time does not work. When the child is hungry he will cry, he himself lets you know. There is no need to look at the clock. The child has his inner body clock. But you go on ruining his clock. And each child will feel hunger differently. One will feel it in four hours, another in three, another in two hours. Now it is a great problem, a rule has been established —the rule of the average.

Beware of the rule of averages. The body has its own inner clock.

. . .

Listen to the body. Follow the body. Never in any way try to dominate the body. The body is your foundation. Once you have started understanding your body, 99 percent of your miseries will simply disappear. But you don't listen.

From the very childhood we have been distracted from the body, we have been taken away from the body. The child is crying, the child is hungry and the mother is looking at the clock. She is not looking at the child. If the child is not given food right now you have distracted him from the body. Instead of giving him food you give him a pacifier. Now you are cheating and you are deceiving. And you are giving something false, plastic, and you are trying to distract and destroy the sensitivity of the body. The wisdom of the body is not allowed to have its say, the mind is entering in.

The child is pacified by the pacifier, he falls asleep. Now the clock says three hours are over and you have to give the milk to the child. Now the child is fast asleep, now his body is sleeping; you wake him up. You again destroy his rhythm. Slowly, slowly you disturb his whole being. A moment comes when he has lost all track of his body. He does not know what his body wants—whether the body wants to eat or not eat, he does not know; whether the body wants to make love or not, he does not know. Everything is manipulated by something from the outside.

ALLOWING THE CHILD TO CRY

From the very beginning the child wants to cry, to laugh. The crying is a deep necessity in him. Through crying, every day he goes through catharsis.

The child has many frustrations. This is bound to be; it is of necessity. The child wants something but he cannot say what, he cannot express it. The child wants something, but the parents may not be in a position to fulfill it. The mother may not be available there. She may be engaged in some other work, and he may not be cared for. At that moment no attention is paid to him, so he starts crying. The mother wants to persuade him, to console him because she is disturbed, the father is disturbed, the whole family is disturbed. No one wants him to cry, crying is a disturbance; everyone tries to distract him so that he might not cry. We can bribe him. The mother can give him a toy; the mother can give him milk—anything to create a distraction or to console him, but he should not cry.

But crying is a deep necessity. If he can cry and is allowed to cry, he will become fresh again; the frustration is thrown through crying. Otherwise, with a stopped crying, the frustration is stopped. Now he will go on piling it up, and you are a "piled-up" cry. Now psychologists say that you need a primal scream. Now a therapy has developed in the West just to help you to scream so totally that every cell of your body is involved in it. If you can scream so madly that your whole body screams in it, you will be relieved of much pain, much suffering that is accumulated.

TOILET TRAINING

Great damage can happen with the toilet training when children are forced to go to the toilet at a certain time. Now, children cannot control their bowel movements; it takes time, it takes years for them to come to a control. So what do they do? They simply force, they simply close their anal mechanism, and because of this they become anally fixated.

That's why so much constipation exists in the world. It is only man who suffers from constipation. No animal suffers from constipation; in the wild state no animal suffers from constipation. Constipation is more psychological; it is a damage to the energy system of the body. And because of constipation many other things grow into the human mind.

A man becomes a hoarder—a hoarder of knowledge, hoarder of money, hoarder of virtue—becomes a hoarder and becomes miserly. He cannot leave anything! Whatsoever he grabs, he holds it. And with this anal emphasis, a great damage happens.

WHEN THE CHILD IS ILL

From the very beginning, from the very childhood, one thing almost always goes wrong, and that is that whenever a child is ill he is paid more attention. This creates a wrong association: the mother loves him more, the father takes care of him more; the whole family puts him in the center, he becomes the most important person. Nobody bothers about a child otherwise—if he is well and okay, it's as if he is not. When he is ill he becomes dictatorial, he dictates his terms. Once this trick is learned—that whenever you are ill you become in some way special—then everybody has to pay attention, because if they are not paying attention you can make them feel guilty. And nobody can say anything to you, because nobody can say that you are responsible for your illness.

If the child is doing something wrong you can say, "You are responsible." But if he is ill you cannot say anything, because illness is not in any way concerned with him—what can he do? But you don't know the facts: 99 percent of illnesses are self-created, generated by yourself to attract attention, affection, significance. And a child learns the trick very easily, because the basic problem for the child is that he is helpless. The basic problem he feels continuously is that he is powerless and everybody is powerful. But when he is ill he becomes powerful and everybody is powerless. He comes to understand it.

A child is very sensitive about knowing things. He comes to know that, "Even Father is nothing, Mother is nothing—nobody is anything before me when I am ill." Then illness becomes something very meaningful, an investment. Whenever he feels neglected in life, whenever he feels, "I am helpless," he will get into illness, he will create it. And this is the problem, a deep problem, because what can you do? When a child is ill everybody has to pay attention.

But now psychologists suggest that whenever a child is ill, take care of him but don't pay too much attention to him. He should be taken care of medically, but not psychologically. Don't create any association in his mind that illness pays; otherwise his whole life, whenever he feels something is wrong he will become ill. Then the wife cannot say anything, then nobody can blame him because he is ill. And everybody has to pity him and give affection.

THE THREE STAGES OF SEX

The first stage is autosexual.

When the child is born he is a narcissist. He loves his body tremendously, and it is beautiful; he knows only his body. Just sucking his own thumb, and he is in such euphoria. You see the child sucking his own thumb—what euphoria is on his face, just playing with his own body, trying to take his toe into his mouth, making a circle of the energy. When the child takes his toe into the mouth a circle is created and the energy starts moving in a circle. The energy circulates naturally in the child and he enjoys, because when the light circulates there is great joy inside.

The child plays with his own sexual organs not knowing they are sexual organs. He has not yet been conditioned; he knows his body as one whole. And certainly, the sexual organs are the most sensitive part of his body. He utterly enjoys touching them, playing with them.

And here is where the society enters into the psyche of the child: "Don't touch!" "Don't" is the first dirty, four-letter word. And out of this one four-letter word, then many more come: can't, won't—these are all four-letter words. Once the child is told "Don't!" by the angry parent, mother or father, and those eyes . . . And the child's hand is taken away from his genital organs, which are naturally very enjoyable. He really enjoys it, and he is not being sexual or anything. It is just the most sensitive part of his body, the most alive part of his body, that's all.

But our conditioned minds . . . he is touching a sexual organ; that is bad, we take his hand away. We create guilt in the child.

Now we have started destroying his natural sexuality. Now we have started poisoning the original source of his joy, of his being. Now we are creating hypocrisy in him; he will become a diplomat. When the parents are there he will not play with his sexual organs. Now the first lie has entered; he cannot be true. Now he knows that if he is true to himself, if he respects himself, if he respects his own joy, if he respects his own instinct, then the parents are angry.

The child is the most exploited phenomenon in the world. No other class has been so exploited as the child. He cannot do anything: he cannot make unions to fight with the parents, he cannot go to the court, he cannot go to the government. He has no way to protect himself against the parental attack.

The first trauma has happened. Now the child will never be able to accept his sexuality naturally, joyously. Some part of the body is not acceptable, some part of the body is ugly, some part of the body is unworthy to be part of his body; he rejects it. Deep down in his psychology he starts castrating himself, and the energy recoils. Energy will not be flowing as naturally as it used to flow before this "don't" happened.

This is the autosexual state: many people remain stuck there. That's why so much masturbation continues all over the world. It is a natural state. It would have passed on its own, it was a growing phase, but the parents disturbed the energy's growing phase.

Once he has started masturbating, it may become a habit, a mechanical habit, and then he will never move to the second stage. He may remain stuck at this stage, which is very childish. He will never attain to full grown-up sexuality. He will never come to know the blissfulness that can come only to a grown-up sexual being. And the irony is that these are the same people who condemn masturbation and make much fuss about it. They have been telling people that if you masturbate you will go blind, if you masturbate you will become a zombie, if you masturbate you will never be intelligent, you will remain stupid. Now all the scientific findings are agreed upon one point: that masturbation never harms anybody. But these suggestions harm people.

If the child is allowed the natural phase of autosexuality, he moves on his own to the second phase, the homosexual—but very few people move to the second phase. The majority remain with the first phase. Even while making love to a woman or a man you may not be doing anything else but just a mutual masturbation.

The second phase is homosexual. Few people move to the second phase; it is a natural phase. The child loves his body. If the child is a boy, he loves a boy's body, his body. To jump to a woman's body, to a girl's body, would be too much of a big gap. Naturally, first he moves in love with other boys; or if the child is a girl, the first natural instinct is to love other girls because they have the same kind of body, the same kind of being. She can understand the girls better than the boys; boys are a world apart.

The homosexual phase is a natural phase. There society helps people to remain stuck again, because it creates barriers between man and woman, girls and boys. If those barriers are not there, then soon the homosexual phase fades away; the interest starts happening in the other sex. But for that, society does not give chances. In the colleges they have to live in separate hostels. Their meeting, their being together, is not accepted.

Homosexuality is perpetuated by the society and condemned by the same society. These strategies have to be understood. The same society condemns the homosexual, calls him perverted, criminal. There are still countries where homosexuality is punished, you can be sent to jail for years. And it is the same society that creates it!

And the third phase is heterosexual.

When a man is really out of autosexuality, homosexuality, then he is capable and mature to fall in love with a woman—which is a totally different world, a different chemistry, a different psychology, a different spirituality. Then he is able to play with this different world, this different organism.

3

conditioning

Does a child not have as much right to privacy and freedom from parental conditioning as the parents expect for themselves? It is one of the most fundamental problems facing humanity today. The future depends on how we solve it. It has never been encountered before. For the first time man has come of age, a certain maturity has happened—and as you become mature you have to face new problems.

Slowly, slowly, as man progressed, he became aware of many kinds of slavery. Only recently in the West have we become aware that the greatest slavery is that of the child. It was never thought of before; it is not mentioned in any scripture of the world. Who could have thought . . . a child and a slave? A slave to his own parents, who love him, who sacrifice themselves for the child? It would have looked ridiculous, utter nonsense! But now, as psychological insight has deepened into the human mind and its functioning, it has become absolutely clear that the child is the most exploited person; nobody has been exploited more than the child. And of course he is being exploited behind a facade of love.

And I don't say that the parents are aware that they are exploiting the child, that they are imposing a slavery on the child, that they are destroying the child, that they are making him stupid, unintelligent, that their whole effort of conditioning the child as a Hindu, as a Mohammedan, as a Christian, as a Buddhist, is inhuman; they are not aware of it, but that does not make any difference as far as the facts are concerned. The child is being conditioned by the parents in ugly ways, and of course the child is helpless: he depends on the parents. He cannot rebel, he cannot escape, he cannot protect himself. He is absolutely vulnerable; hence he can be easily exploited.

Parental conditioning is the greatest slavery in the world. It has to be completely uprooted, only then will man be able for the first time to be really free, truly free, authentically free, because the child is the father of the man. If the child is brought up in a wrong way then the whole of humanity goes wrong. The child is the seed: if the seed itself is poisoned and corrupted by well-intentioned people, well-wishing people, then there is no hope for a free human individual. Then that dream can never be fulfilled.

What you think you have is not individuality, it is only personality. It is something cultivated in you, in your nature, by your parents, the society, the priest, the politician, the educators. The educator, from the kindergarten to the university, is in the service of the vested interests, of the establishment. His whole purpose is to destroy every child in such a way, to cripple every child in such a way that he adjusts to the established society. There is a fear. The fear is that if the child is left unconditioned from the very beginning he will be so intelligent, he will be so alert, aware, that his whole lifestyle will be of rebellion. And nobody wants rebels; everybody wants obedient people.

Parents love the obedient child. And remember, the obedient child is almost always the most stupid child. The rebellious child is the intelligent one, but he is not respected or loved. The teachers don't love him, the society does not give him respect; he is condemned. Either he has to compromise with the society or he has to live in a kind of self-guilt. Naturally, he feels that he has not been good to his parents, he has not made them happy.

Remember perfectly well, the parents of Jesus were not happy with Jesus; the parents of Gautam the Buddha were not happy with Gautam the Buddha. These people were so intelligent, so rebellious, how could their parents be happy with them? And each child is born with such great possibilities and potential that if he is allowed and helped to develop his individuality without any hindrance from others we will have a beautiful world, we will have a tremendous variety of geniuses. The genius happens very rarely not because the genius is rarely born, no; the genius rarely happens because it is very difficult to escape from the conditioning process of the society. Only once in a while does a child somehow manage to escape from its clutches.

Every child is being enveloped—by the parents, by the society, by the teachers, by the priests, by all the vested interests—enveloped in many layers of conditioning. He is given a certain religious ideology; it is not his choice. And whenever somebody is forced with no choice of his own you are crippling the person, you are destroying his intelligence. You are not giving him a chance to choose, you are not allowing him to function intelligently; you are managing it in such a way that he will function only mechanically. He will be a Christian, but he is not Christian by choice. And what does it mean to be a Christian if it is not your choice?

The few people who followed Jesus, who went with him, were courageous people. They were the only Christians: they risked their lives, they went against the current, they lived dangerously; they were ready to die, but they were not ready to compromise. The few people who went with Gautam Buddha were real Buddhists. But now there are millions of Christians around the world and millions of Buddhists around the world and they are all bogus, they are pseudo. They are bound to be pseudo—it is forced on them! They are enveloped in a certain religious ideology, then they are enveloped in a certain political ideology—they are told that they are Indians, that they are Iranians, that they are Chinese, that they are Germans; a certain nationality is imposed on them. Humanity is one, the earth is one! But the politicians wouldn't like it to be one because if the earth is one then the politicians with all their politics have to disappear. Then where will all these presidents and prime ministers go? They can exist only if the world remains divided.

Religion is one, but then what will happen to the pope, to all the stupid shankaracharyas, all the ayatollahs? What will happen to all these people? They can exist only if there are many religions, many churches, many cults, many creeds. There are three hundred religions on the earth and at least three thousand sects of these religions. Then of course there is a possibility for many priests, bishops, archbishops, high priests, shankaracharyas to exist. This possibility will disappear.

And I tell you, religiousness is one! It has nothing to do with any Bible, any Veda, any Gita. It has something to do with a loving heart, with an intelligent being. It has something to do with awareness, meditativeness. But then all the vested interests will suffer.

Hence parents who belong to a certain establishment, a certain nation, a certain church, a certain denomination, are bound to force their ideas on the children. And the strange thing is that the children are always more intelligent than the parents, because the parents belong to the past and the children belong to the future. The parents are already conditioned, enveloped, covered. Their mirrors are covered with so much dust that they don't reflect anything; they are blind.

Only a blind man can be a Hindu or a Mohammedan or a Jaina or a Christian. A man with eyes is simply religious. He does not go to the church or to the temple or to the mosque; he will not worship all kinds of stupid images. All kinds of gods, all kinds of superstitions! Parents carry all these. When a child is born he is a clean slate, a tabula rasa; nothing is written on him. That's his beauty: the mirror is without any dust. He can see more clearly.

Mom: "Jimmy, did you fall over with your new trousers on?"

Jimmy: "Yes, Mom, there wasn't time to take them off."

The first-grade teacher was talking to her class about nature and she called it "The World Around You." She asked little Helen in the first row, "Now, Helen tell everyone in the class. Are you animal, vegetable, or mineral?"

"I'm not any of those," she replied promptly. "I'm a real live girl!"

A little fellow who was fishing off the end of a pier lost his balance while trying to land a fish and fell in the lake. Several men who were also fishing nearby rushed to his aid and pulled him out.

"How did you come to fall in?" one of the men asked him.

"I didn't come to fall in," the kid said. "I came to fish!"

A large family was finally able to move into a more spacious home. Sometime later an uncle asked his nephew, "How do you like your new house?"

"Just fine," replied the lad. "My brother and I have our own rooms and so do my sisters. But poor Mom, she's still stuck in the same room with Dad!"

Every child is born intelligent, clear, clean, but we start heaping rubbish on him.

He has much more right than the parents because he is beginning his life. The parents are already burdened, they are already crippled, they are already depending on crutches. He has more right to be his own self. He needs privacy, but parents don't allow him any privacy; they are very afraid of the child's privacy. They are continuously poking their noses into the child's affairs; they want to have their say about everything.

The child needs privacy because all that is beautiful grows in privacy. Remember it: it is one of the most fundamental laws of life. The roots grow underground; if you take them out of the ground they start dying. They need privacy, absolute privacy. The child grows in the mother's womb in darkness, in privacy. If you bring the child into the light, among the public, he will die. He needs nine months of absolute privacy. Everything that needs growth needs privacy. A grown-up person does not need as much privacy because he is already grown up, but a child needs much more privacy. But he is not left alone at all.

Parents are very worried whenever they see that the child is missing or is alone; they immediately become concerned. They are afraid, because if the child is alone he will start developing his individuality. He always has to be kept within limits so that the parents can go on watching, because their very watching does not allow his individuality to grow; their watching covers him, envelops him with a personality.

Personality is nothing but an envelope. It comes from a beautiful word, *persona*; persona means a mask. In Greek dramas the actors used masks. *Sona* means sound, *per* means through. They used to speak through the mask; you could not see their real faces, you could only hear their voices. Hence the mask was called a *persona* because the sound was heard through it, and out of persona comes the word *personality*.

The child has to be continuously on guard because he is being watched. You can see it yourself: if you are taking a bath you are a totally different person. In your bathroom you can put aside your mask; even grown-up people who are very serious start singing, humming. Even grown-up people start making faces in the mirror! You are in private, you are perfectly aware that you have locked the door—but if you suddenly become aware that somebody is watching through the keyhole, an immediate change will happen to you. You will again become serious, the song will disappear, you will not be making faces in the mirror; you will start behaving as you are supposed to behave. This is the personality—you are back in the envelope.

A child needs immense privacy, as much as possible, a maximum of privacy so that he can develop his individuality with no interference. But we are trespassing on the child, continuously trespassing. The parents are continuously asking, "What are you doing? What are you thinking?" Even thinking! They even want to look in your mind.

There are a few tribes in the Far East where each child has to tell his dreams every morning to the parents, because even in the dreams he cannot be left alone. He may be dreaming wrong dreams, he may be thinking things he should not think; the parents have to be reported to. The early morning ritual is that first thing before breakfast he has to relate his dreams, what he has seen in the night.

Psychoanalysis is a very late development in the West, but in the East, in these Far Eastern tribes, psychoanalysis has been practiced by the parents for thousands of years. And of course the poor child does not know the symbology so he simply relates the dream as it is. He does not know what it means; only the parents know. But this is going too far. It is encroaching upon him, it is inhuman; it is overlapping on somebody's space.

Just because the child is dependent on you for food, for clothes, for shelter, do you think you have the right to do it? Because if the child says that he has seen that he was flying in his dream, the parents immediately know that that is a sexual dream. Now they will curb his behavior more, they will discipline him more. They will give him an early morning cold bath! They will teach him more about celibacy and they will teach him that, "If you are not celibate things will go wrong. If you think about sexuality you will lose all intelligence, you will go blind," and all kinds of nonsense.

A child needs immense privacy. The parents should come only to help him, not to interfere. He should be allowed to do things or not to do things. Parents should only be alert that he does not do any harm to himself or to anybody else—that's enough. More than that is ugly.

A tourist drove into a small town and spoke to a boy who was sitting on a bench in front of the post office.

"How long have you lived here?" the tourist asked.

"About twelve years," the boy replied.

"It sure is an out-of-the-way place, isn't it?" the tourist asked.

"It sure is," the boy said.

"There isn't much going on," the tourist said. "I don't see anything here to keep you busy."

"Neither do I," the boy said. "That's why I like it."

The children like very much to be left alone; spaciousness is needed for their growth. Yes, parents have to be alert, cautious, so that no harm happens to the child, but this is a negative kind of cautiousness—they are not to interfere positively. They have to give the child a great longing to inquire about truth, but they have not to give him an ideology that gives him the idea of truth. They should not teach him about truth, they should teach him how to inquire about truth. Inquiry should be taught, investigation should be taught, adventure should be taught. The children should be helped so that they can ask questions, and the parents should not answer those questions unless they really know. And even if they know they should say it as Buddha used to say it to his disciples: "Don't believe in what I say! This is my experience, but the moment I say it to you it becomes false because for you it is not an experience. Listen to me, but don't believe. Experiment, inquire, search. Unless you yourself know, your knowledge is of no use; it is dangerous. A knowledge which is borrowed is a hindrance."

But that's what parents go on doing: they go on conditioning the child.

No conditioning is needed for the children, no direction has to be given to them. They have to be helped to be themselves, they have to be supported, nourished, strengthened. A real father, a real mother, real parents will be a blessing to the child. The child will feel helped by them so that he becomes more rooted in his nature, more grounded, more centered, so that he starts loving himself rather than feeling guilty about himself, so that he respects himself.

Remember, unless a person loves himself he cannot love anybody else in the world, unless a child respects himself he cannot respect anybody else. That's why all your love is bogus and all your respect is pseudo, phony. You don't respect yourself, how can you respect anybody else? Unless love for yourself is born within your being it will not radiate to others. First you have to become a light unto yourself, then your light will spread, will reach others.

It was examination day at school and a bad-tempered teacher was questioning a small boy about his knowledge of plants and flowers. The boy was unable to answer any question correctly. In frustration, the teacher turned to his assistant and shouted, "Go and bring me a handful of hay!"

As the assistant turned to go out, the small boy cried, "And for me, just a small coffee, please!"

A man was driving along a country road when his car broke down. While he was fixing it, a small boy approached and asked, "What is that?"

"It's a jack," said the man.

"My father has two of those," said the boy.

Then a minute later he asked again, "And what is that?"

"That's a flashlight."

"Oh, my father has two of those too. And over there? Is that a spanner?"

"Yes," said the man, irritably.

"My father has two of those."

The conversation went on in this vein for some time. Finally the repair was finished and the man got up and went to piss at the side of the road. As he was pissing he pointed to his reproductive machinery and asked, "Does your father have two of these too?"

"Of course not!" said the boy. "But he has one that is twice as long!"

Children are immensely intelligent, they just need a chance! They need opportunities to grow, the right climate. Every child is born with the potential of enlightenment, with the potential of becoming awakened, but we destroy it. This has been the greatest calamity in the whole history of man. No other slavery has been as bad as the slavery of the child and no other slavery has taken as much juice out of humanity as the slavery of the child, and this is also going to be the most difficult task for humanity to get rid of it. Unless we arrange the whole of society in a totally different way, unless a radical change happens and the family disappears and gives place to a commune, it will not be possible.

Once this old pattern of family disappears into a more multidimensional set-up, humanity can have a new birth. A new man is needed and the new man will bring the very paradise that in the past we were hoping for in some other life. Paradise can be here-now, but we have to bring about a new child.

Why do people voluntarily repress themselves and adopt crippling defense mechanisms?

For survival. The child is so fragile he cannot exist on his own. You can exploit this. You can force the child to learn anything you want him to—that's what a behaviorist like B.F. Skinner goes on doing in his lab. He teaches pigeons to play Ping-Pong, but the trick is the same: reward and punishment. If they play they are rewarded; if they don't play, if they are reluctant, they are punished. If they make a right move they are rewarded, given food; if they make a wrong move they are given an electric shock. Even pigeons start learning Ping-Pong.

That's what has always been done in the circus. You can go and see. Even lions, beautiful lions, are caged, and elephants are moving according to the whip of the ringmaster. They have been starved and then they are rewarded—punished and rewarded—this is the whole trick.

What you do in the circus with the animals you go on doing with your children. But you do it very unconsciously because it has been done to you; this is the only way you know how to train and bring up children. This is what you call "bringing up." In fact, it is bringing down; it is forcing them into a lower existence rather than bringing them up to a higher existence. These are all Skinnerian tricks and techniques—because of them we voluntarily start repressing ourselves and adopt crippling defense mechanisms.

A child does not know what is right and what is wrong. We teach him. We teach him according to our mind. The same thing may be right in Tibet and wrong in India; the same thing may be right in your house and wrong in your neighbor's house. But you force it onto the child: "This is right, you have to do it." The child gets approval when he does it and gets disapproval when he does not do it. When he follows you, you are happy and you pat the child; when he does not follow you, you are angry and you torture the child, you beat the child, you starve the child, you don't give your love to him.

Naturally the child starts understanding that his survival is at stake. If he listens to this mother and this father all is okay; if not, they will kill him. And what can the child do? How can he assert himself against these powerful people? They loom large. They are huge and powerful and they can do anything.

By the time the child becomes powerful he is already conditioned. Then the conditioning has gone so deep in him that now there is no need for the father and mother to follow him. The inner conditioning, what they call the conscience, will go on torturing him.

For example, if the child starts playing with his genitals—which is a joy to children, a natural joy, because the child's body is very sensitive—it is not sexual at all in the sense that you understand sexuality. The child is really very, very alive, and naturally when the child is alive his genitals are more alive than other parts of the body. That is where life energy accumulates—it is the most sensitive part. Touching and playing with the genitals the child feels tremendously happy—but you are afraid. It is your problem.

You start being afraid that he is masturbating or something. It is nothing. It is sheer joy at playing with one's body. It is not masturbation or anything, it is loving one's body.

It is your guilt, your fear. Somebody may see that your son is doing this and what will they think of how you are bringing up your children? "Make them civilized, teach them not to do that!" So you stop it, you shout at the child. You say, "Stop!" again and again and again, and it goes deeper, deeper, deeper, and becomes a "conscience," an unconscious part of the child. Now there is no need for you. When he starts playing with his genitals something from the inside will say, "Stop!" and he will become afraid—maybe the father is looking or the mother is looking—and he will feel guilty. And then we teach him that there is God the Father who is always looking everywhere, even in the bathroom. He goes on watching you everywhere. This concept of God is crippling; then you are not free even in your bathroom! Nowhere are you free, that omnipotent God follows you like a detective wherever you are. When you are making love to a woman he is standing there. He won't allow you. He is a super-policeman—in addition to the conscience that the parents have created.

That's why Buddha says that unless you kill your parents you will never become free. Killing the parents means killing the voice of the parent inside you, killing the conscience inside you, dropping these nonsense ideas and starting to live your own life according to your own consciousness. Remember, *consciousness* has to be more and *conscience* has to be less. By and by, conscience has to disappear completely and pure consciousness has to be lived.

Consciousness is the law—let consciousness be the only law. Then whatsoever you feel, it is your life. You have to decide. It is nobody else's life; nobody else has any right to decide. I am not saying that you will always be doing right—sometimes you will do wrong. But that too is part of your freedom and part of your growth. Many times you will go astray but that is perfectly all right—going astray is a way of coming back home. A person who never goes astray never comes back home, he is already dead. A person who never does anything wrong never enjoys doing anything right. He is just a slave. A mental slavery is created.

A human child is dependent on his parents for a long time—at least twenty-one to twenty-five years. It is a long time, almost one-third of his whole life. For a third of his life he is being conditioned. Just think—twenty-five years of conditioning! Anything can be forced on a person. And once you learn these tricks it is very difficult to forget them.

That's why it is so difficult to take a jump into reality and start living your life. Of course, in the beginning it will be very shaky; you will tremble many times, because naturally you will be going against your parents, you will be going against the society. Society is your parents' writ large; your parents were nothing but agents of this society. It is all a conspiracy—the parents, the teachers, the policeman, the magistrate, the president—it is all a conspiracy, they are all together and they are all holding the future of all children.

Once you have learned, unlearning becomes very difficult because after twenty-five years of constant repetition you are completely hypnotized. A de-hypnosis is needed; you have to drop all this conditioning.

Yes, it is simply survival, the need to survive. The child wants to live, that's why he starts compromising. He bargains. Anybody will bargain when there is a question of life and death. If you are dying in a desert and somebody has water and you are thirsty and you are dying, he can ask any price. He can manage anything, he can force anything upon you. That's what we have done up to now with children.

You ask, "Why do people voluntarily repress themselves and

adopt crippling defense mechanisms?" It is not voluntary. It looks as if it is voluntary because by the time you become alert it is almost inside your blood and bones. But it is not voluntary, no child ever learns anything voluntarily—it is forced, it is violent.

You can watch any child. Every child resists, every child fights to the very end, every child creates trouble for the parents, every child tries hard this way and that to escape from this crippling mechanism. But finally the parents get hold of him because they are more powerful. It is simply a question of the powerful and the powerless.

So it is not unnatural that when children start to grow up they start taking revenge on the parents. That reaction is natural. It is very difficult to forgive your parents—that's why all societies teach you to respect them. If you cannot forgive them at least respect them; if you cannot love them, at least respect them. But that respect is formal, bogus. Deep down you remain angry.

If what I am saying is heard, if what I am saying becomes prevalent in the world someday, then children will really love their parents. Then children will be really in tune with their parents because the parents will not be enemies to them, they will be friends.

. . .

The human child is the weakest child in the whole of existence. His weakness is a blessing in disguise, but it can also be exploited—and that's what has been done down the centuries. The parents never allowed the weakness, helplessness, and dependence of the child to turn into independence, strength, integrity, individuality; they were determined that the child should remain obedient—naturally, because an obedient child is not a trouble. A disobedient child is a continuous trouble. But a disobedient child is a real human being.

The obedient child is just simple cow dung. A child who cannot say no has no integrity. And if a child cannot say no to something, his yes is meaningless. The yes has meaning only when the child is capable of saying no, too. Then it is up to his intelligence to decide. But it is easier for parents that a child always says yes. He is rewarded for being obedient and he is punished for being disobedient. And the situation is the same in the schools. Teachers want you to be obedient; it is easier for them to control you, to dominate you.

All my teachers were complaining to my father, and my father was telling them, "Who am I to complain to? Do you think I am in power? Do you think he is going to listen to me? Do whatsoever you want to do: punish him, expel him from the school—whatsoever you want to do, I absolutely agree to it. But don't bother me about him, because the whole day people are coming to me . . . have I nothing else to do? Or have I just to go on listening to what he has done to this teacher, that teacher, this neighbor, that neighbor?"

And he told me, "You can do anything you want, but don't spoil my business. Everybody is coming into the shop, and at first I think they are customers . . . but it turns out they are your customers."

I suggested to my father, "You do one thing. In your big shop, just in the corner you can write on a small board COMPLAINTS HERE in the back. You are saved from the trouble, and I will see those people. Let them come to me."

He said, "The idea is good, but have you seen in any shop a complaints box? People will think those complaints are against me and the shop; nobody will think they are against you. And you will play more mischief on those poor guys who have come in to complain."

I said, "It was just a suggestion to help you."

It is difficult for parents, it is difficult for teachers, it is difficult for priests; it is difficult for everybody to allow any kind of disobedience. Even God—who is omnipotent, all-powerful, the greatest despot, the greatest dictator—could not allow it; even he could not tolerate a little disobedience from Adam and Eve. They were thrown out of the Garden of Eden and they had committed no sin. In fact, since hearing that it was an apple tree I have been eating apples as much as possible. I don't see any sin arising out of eating the fruit from an apple tree.

But the question was not the apple tree.

The question was disobedience.

So the first thing is that obedience has to be forced; for obedience, fear has to be used. That fear becomes in religious terms, hell. For obedience, reward has to be used; in religious terms, that becomes paradise or heaven. And to keep control over everything a father figure is needed—so God becomes the father.

I know why they have not made God a mother. I know from my own experience that my mother would hide me in the house when my father was very angry and searching for me because I had done something. When my father would refuse to give me any money because I had done something that he had prohibited, my mother would manage to give me money. So I know that a mother cannot be such a disciplinarian as a father can be.

And a mother can be persuaded very easily, because she is nothing but love, she is nothing but heart. The father is head, logic, reason, discipline. The father is a man, and the society is man-made. My mother even used to enjoy it when I would come and say to her, "I have done something, and I am in urgent need of help."

She would say, "But first tell me what you have done. I will save you, I will try my best, but first tell me the whole story. You bring such juicy stories that I wonder why your father gets angry. He should enjoy them."

The priests, the father in heaven, the parents here on the earth, the teachers, the political leaders, they all want absolute obedience from everybody so that there is no question of any rebellion, no change, so their vested interests are protected. We have all become victims of their vested interests. It is time that things should be changed.

The obedient child is always mediocre; to be disobedient means a little intelligence is needed. The obedient child becomes a good citizen, goes to the church every Sunday; the disobedient child is unreliable. What will he do in his life? He may become a painter, he may become a musician, he may become a dancer—which are not very profitable professions—or he may become just nobody, a vagabond, enjoying his freedom.

I want you to jump out of this circle. Drop all fear. There is nothing to fear. There is no hell to be worried about and there is no paradise for which you have to be greedy.

Paradise is here. And if we drop the idea of paradise beyond death, we can make this paradise a thousandfold more beautiful.

4

parenting the new child

If you look at the faces of children when they arrive, fresh from the very source of life, you will see a certain presence which cannot be named—unnameable, indefinable.

The child is alive. You cannot define this aliveness but it is there, you can feel it. It is so much there that howsoever blind you are you cannot miss it. It is fresh. You can smell the freshness around a child. That fragrance slowly, slowly disappears. And if unfortunately the child becomes successful—a celebrity, a president, a prime minister, a pope—then the same child stinks. He had come with a tremendous fragrance, immeasurable, indefinable, unnameable. Look into the eyes of a child—you cannot find anything deeper. The eyes of a child are an abyss, there is no bottom to them. Unfortunately, the way society will destroy him, soon his eyes will be only superficial; because of layers and layers of conditioning, that depth, that immense depth will have disappeared long before. And that was his original face.

The child has no thoughts. About what can he think? Thinking needs a past, thinking needs problems. He has no past, he has only future. He has no problems yet, he is without problems. There is no possibility of thinking for him. What can he think?

The child is conscious but without thoughts. This is the original face of the child.

Once this was your face too, and although you have forgotten it, it is still there within you, waiting someday to be rediscovered. I am saying rediscovered because you have discovered it many times in your previous lives, and again and again you go on forgetting it.

Perhaps even in this life there have been moments when you have come very close to knowing it, to feeling it, to being it. But the world is too much with us. Its pull is great, and there are a thousand and one directions the world is pulling you. It is pulling you in so many directions that you are falling apart. It is a miracle how people go on managing to keep themselves together. Otherwise one hand will be going to the north, another hand to the south, their head must be going toward heaven; all their parts will be flying all over the place. It is certainly a miracle how you go on keeping yourself together. Perhaps the pressure from all sides is so great that your hands and legs and heads cannot fly. You are pressed in from everywhere.

Even if by chance you happen to meet your original face, you will not be able to recognize it, it will be such a stranger. Perhaps you come across it once in a while, just by accident, but you don't even say hi! It is a stranger and perhaps deep down, a certain fear that is always there with every stranger.

You are asking how we can save the original face of our children. You don't have to do anything directly; anything done directly will be a disturbance. You have to learn the art of nondoing.

That is a very difficult art. It is not something that you have to do to protect or to save the original face of the child. Whatever you do will distort the original face. You have to learn nondoing; you have to learn to keep away, out of the way of the child. You have to be very courageous because it is risky to leave the child to himself.

For thousands of years we have been told that if the child is left to himself he will be a savage. That is sheer nonsense. I am sitting before you—do you think I am a savage? And I have lived without being interfered with by my parents. Yes, there was much trouble for them and there will be much trouble for you too, but it is worth it. The original face of the child is so valuable that any trouble is worth it. It is so priceless that whatsoever you have to pay for it, it is still cheap; you are getting it for nothing. And the joy on the day you find your child with his original face intact, with the same beauty that he had brought into the world, the same innocence, the same clarity, the same joyfulness, cheerfulness, the same aliveness . . . What more can you hope for?

You cannot give anything to the child, you can only take. If you really want to give a gift to the child, this is the only gift possible: don't interfere. Take the risk and let the child go into the unknown, into the uncharted.

It is difficult. Great fear grips the parents: Who knows what will happen to the child? Out of this fear they start molding a certain pattern of life for the child. Out of fear they start directing him into a particular way, toward a particular goal, but they don't know that because of their fear they are killing the child. He will never be blissful. And he will never be grateful to you; he will always carry a grudge against you.

Sigmund Freud has a great insight in this matter: He says, "Every culture respects the father. No culture on earth exists, or has ever existed, which has not propounded, propagated the idea that the father has to be respected." Sigmund Freud says, "This respect for the father arises because some time back in prehistoric times the father must have been killed by the children just to save themselves from being crippled."

It is a strange idea, but very significant. He is saying that the respect is being paid to the father out of guilt, and that guilt has been carried for thousands of years. Somewhere . . . it is not a historical fact, but a meaningful myth, that young people must have killed their fathers and then repented—naturally, because he was their father. But he was driving them into ways of living where they were not happy. They killed him, but then they repented. Then they started worshipping the spirits of the ancestors, fathers, forefathers, out of fear, because the ghosts of those ancestors can take revenge. And then slowly, slowly, it became a convention to be respectful toward the elders. But why?

I would like you to be respectful to the children. The children deserve all the respect you can manage because they are so fresh, so innocent, so close to godliness. It is time to pay respect to them, not to force them to pay respect to all kinds of corrupted people— cunning, crooked, full of shit—just because they are old. I would like to reverse the whole thing: respect the children because they are closer to the source; you are far away. They are still original, you are already a carbon copy. And do you understand what it can do if you are respectful to children? Then through love and respect you can save them from going in any wrong direction, not out of fear but out of your respect and love.

My grandfather . . . I could not speak a lie to my grandfather because he respected me so much. When the whole family was against me I could at least depend on the old man. He would not bother about all the proofs that were against me. He would say, "I don't care what he has done. If he has done it, it must be right. I know him, he cannot do wrong."

And when he was with me, of course the whole family had to defer to him. I would tell him the whole thing, and he would say, "There is no need to be worried. Do whatsoever you feel is right, because who else can decide? In your situation, in your place, only you can decide. Do whatsoever you feel is right, and always remember that I am here to support you because I not only love you, I respect you too."

His respect toward me was the greatest treasure I could have received. When he was dying I was eighty miles away. He informed me that I should come immediately because there was not much time. I came quickly; within two hours I was there. It was as if he was just waiting for me. He opened his eyes and he said, "I was just trying to continue to breathe so that you could reach me. Just one thing I want to say: I will not be here now to support you, and you will need support. But remember, wherever I am, my love and my respect will remain with you. Don't be afraid of anybody, don't be afraid of the world."

Those were his last words:

"Don't be afraid of the world."

Respect the children, make them fearless.

But if you are yourself full of fear, how can you make them fearless?

Don't force them to show respect toward you because you are their father, you are their daddy, their mom, this and that. Change this attitude and see what transformation respect can bring to your children. They will listen to you more carefully if you respect them. They will try to understand you and your mind more carefully if you respect them. They have to. And in no way are you imposing anything; so if by understanding they feel you are right and they follow you, they will not lose their original face.

The original face is not lost by going on a certain way. It is lost by children being forced, forced against their will. Love and respect can sweetly help them to be more understanding about the world, can help them to be more alert, aware, careful—because life is precious, and it is a gift from existence. We should not waste it. At the moment of death we should be able to say that we are leaving the world better, more beautiful, more graceful.

But this is possible only if we leave this world with our original face, the same face with which we came into it.

. . .

According to me, you can do only one thing with your children, and that is share your own life. Tell them that you have been conditioned by your parents, that you have lived within certain limits according to certain ideals, and because of these limits and ideals you have missed life completely, and you don't want to destroy your children's life. You want them to be totally free—free of you, because to them you represent the whole past.

It needs guts and it needs immense love in a father, in a mother, to tell the children, "You need to be free of us. Don't obey us; depend on your own intelligence. Even if you go astray it is far better than to remain a slave and always remain right. It is better to commit mistakes on your own and learn from them, rather than follow somebody else and not commit mistakes. Then you are never going to learn anything except following, and that is poison, pure poison."

It is very easy if you love. Don't ask how, because "how" means you are asking for a method, a methodology, a technique—and love is not a technique.

Love your children, enjoy their freedom. Let them commit mistakes, help them to see where they have committed a mistake. Tell them, "To commit mistakes is not wrong. Commit as many mistakes as possible, because that is the way you will be learning more. But don't commit the same mistake again and again, because that makes you stupid." You will have to figure it out living with your children moment to moment, allowing them every possible freedom in small things.

For example, in my childhood . . . and it has been the same for centuries, the children are being taught, "Go to bed early, and get up early in the morning. That makes you wise."

I told my father, "It seems to be strange: when I am not feeling sleepy, you force me to sleep early in the evening." And in Jaina houses early in the evening is really early, because supper is at five o'clock, at the most six. And then there is nothing else to do, so the children should go to sleep.

I said to him, "When my energy is not ready to go to sleep, you force me to go to sleep. And in the morning, when I am feeling sleepy, you drag me out of the bed. This seems to be a strange way of making me wise! And I don't see the connection—how am I going to become wise by being forced to sleep when I am not feeling sleepy? For hours I lie down in the bed, in the darkness . . . time that would have in some way been used, would have been creative, and you force me to sleep. But sleep is not something in your hands. You cannot just close your eyes and go to sleep. Sleep comes when it comes; it does not follow your order or my order, so for hours I am wasting my time.

"And then in the morning when I am really feeling sleepy, you force me to wake up—five o'clock, early in the morning—and you drag me out for a morning walk to the forest. I am feeling sleepy and you are dragging me. And I don't see how all this is going to make me wise. You please explain it to me! And how many people have become wise through this process? You just show me a few wise people—I don't see anybody around. And I have been talking to my grandfather, and he said that it is all nonsense. Of the whole household, that old man is the only sincere man. He does not care what others will say, but he has told me that it is all nonsense: 'Wisdom does not come by going early to bed. I have been going early to bed my whole life—seventy years—and wisdom has not come yet, and I don't think it is going to come! Now it is time for death to come, not for wisdom. So don't be befooled by these proverbs.'"

I told my father, "You think it over, and please be authentic and true. Give me this much freedom—that I can go to sleep when I feel sleep is coming, and I can get up when I feel that it is time, and sleep is no longer there."

He thought for one day, and the next day he said, "Okay, perhaps you are right. You do it according to yourself. Listen to your body rather than listening to me."

This should be the principle: children should be helped to listen to their bodies, to listen to their own needs. The basic thing for parents is to guard the children from falling into a ditch. The function of their discipline is negative.

Remember the word "negative" . . . no positive programming but only a negative guarding—because children are children, and they can get into something that will harm them, cripple them. Then too don't order them not to go, but explain to them. Don't make it a point of obedience; still let them choose. You simply explain the whole situation. Children are very receptive, and if you are respectful toward them they are ready to listen, ready to understand. Then leave them with their understanding. And it is a question only of a few years in the beginning; soon they will be getting settled in their intelligence and your guarding will not be needed at all. Soon they will be able to move on their own.

I can understand the fear of the parents that the children may go in a direction they don't like—but that is your problem! Your children are not born for your likings and your dislikings. They have to live their life, and you should rejoice that they are living their life, whatever it is.

Whenever you follow your potential, you always become the best. Whenever you go astray from the potential, you remain mediocre.

The whole society consists of mediocre people for the simple reason that nobody is what he was destined to be. He is something else, and whatever he does he cannot be the best and he cannot feel a fulfillment; he cannot rejoice.

So the work of the parents is very delicate, and it is precious because the whole life of the child depends on it. Don't give any positive program. Help him in every possible way that he wants.

For example, I used to climb trees. Now, there are a few trees which are safe to climb; their branches are strong, their trunk is strong. You can go even to the very top, and still there is no need to be afraid that a branch will break. But there are a few trees that are very fragile. Because I used to climb on the trees to get mangoes, or *jamuns,* another beautiful fruit in India, my family was very worried and they would always send somebody to prevent me.

I told my father, "Rather than preventing me, please explain to me which trees are dangerous, so that I can avoid them, and which trees are not dangerous, so that I can climb them. But if you try to prevent me from climbing, there is a danger: I may climb a wrong tree, and the responsibility will be yours. Climbing I am not going to stop, I love it." It is really one of the most beautiful experiences to be on the top of the tree in the sun with the high wind, and the whole tree is dancing—a very nourishing experience.

I said, "I am not going to stop it. Your work is to tell me exactly which trees I should not climb—because I can fall from them, can have fractures, can damage my body. But don't give me a blank order to stop climbing. That I am not going to do." So he had to come with me and go around the town to show me which trees are dangerous. Then I asked him the second question, "Do you know any good climber in the city who can teach me even to climb the dangerous trees?"

He said, "You are too much! Now this is going too far. You had told me, I understood it . . ."

I said, "I will follow it, because I have myself proposed it. But the trees that you are saying are dangerous are irresistible, because *jamun* grows on them. It is really delicious, and when it is ripe I may not be able to resist the temptation. You are my father, it is your duty . . . you must know somebody who can help me."

He said, "If I had known that to be a father was going to be so difficult, I would have never been a father—at least of you! Yes, I know one man," and he introduced me to an old man who was a rare climber, the best.

He was a woodcutter, and he was so old that you could not believe that he could do woodcutting. He did only rare jobs, which nobody else was ready to do . . . big trees that were spreading on the houses, he would cut off the branches. He was just an expert, and he did it without damaging their roots or the houses. First he would tie the branches to other branches with ropes. Then he would cut these branches and then with the ropes pull the other branches away from the house and let them fall on the ground.

And he was so old! But whenever there was some situation like that, when no other woodcutter was ready, he was ready. So my father told him, "Teach him something, particularly about trees which are dangerous, which can break." Branches can break . . . and I had fallen already two, three times—I still carry the marks on my legs.

That old man looked at me and he said, "Nobody has ever come, particularly a father bringing a boy! . . . It is a dangerous thing, but if he loves it, I would love to teach him." And he was teaching me how to manage to climb trees which were dangerous. He showed me all kinds of strategies of how to protect yourself: if you want to go high up the tree and you don't want to fall onto the ground, then first tie yourself with a rope to a point where you feel the tree is strong enough, and then go up. If you fall, you will be hanging from the rope, but you will not fall to the ground. And that really helped me; since then I have not fallen!

The function of a father or a mother is great, because they are bringing a new guest into the world who knows nothing, but who brings some potential in him. And unless his potential grows, he will remain unhappy.

No parents like to think of their children remaining unhappy; they want them to be happy. It is just that their thinking is wrong. They think if they become doctors, if they become professors, engineers, scientists, then they will be happy. They don't know! They can only be happy if they become what they have come to become. They can only become the seed that they are carrying within themselves.

So help in every possible way to give freedom, to give opportunities. Ordinarily, if a child asks a mother anything, without even listening to the child, to what he is asking, the mother simply says no. "No" is an authoritative word; "yes" is not. So neither father nor mother nor anybody else who is in authority wants to say yes, even to any ordinary thing.

The child wants to play outside the house: "No!" The child wants to go out while it is raining and wants to dance in the rain: "No! You will get a cold." A cold is not a cancer, but a child who has been prevented from dancing in the rain has missed something great, something really beautiful. A cold would have been worth the experience—and it is not that he will necessarily catch a cold. In fact the more you protect him, the more he becomes vulnerable. The more you allow him, the more he becomes immune.

Parents have to learn to say yes. In ninety-nine cases when they ordinarily say no, it is for no other reason than simply to show authority. Everybody cannot become the president of the country, cannot have authority over millions of people. But everybody can become a husband, can have authority over his wife; every wife can become a mother, can have authority over the child; every child can have a teddy bear, and have authority over the teddy bear . . .

kick him from this corner to the other corner, give him good slaps, slaps that he really wanted to give to the mother or to the father. And the poor teddy bear has nobody below him.

This is an authoritarian society.

What I am saying is in creating children who have freedom, who have heard "yes" and have rarely heard "no," the authoritarian society will disappear. We will have a more human society.

So it is not only a question of the children. Those children are going to become tomorrow's society: the child is the father of man.

THE SEVEN-YEAR CIRCLES OF LIFE

You will have to understand some significant growth patterns. Life has seven-year cycles: it moves in seven-year circles just as the earth makes one rotation on its axis in twenty-four hours. Now nobody knows why not twenty-five, why not twenty-three. There is no way to answer it; it is simply a fact.

And if you understand those seven-year circles, you will understand a great deal about human growth.

The first seven years are the most important because the foundation of life is being laid. That's why all the religions are very much concerned about grabbing children as quickly as possible. The Jews will circumcise the child. What nonsense! But they are stamping the child as a Jew; that is a primitive way of stamping. You still do it on the cattle around here. I have seen stamps, every owner brands his cattle, otherwise they can get mixed up. It is a cruel thing. Red-hot steel has to be used to stamp the cattle's leather skin. It burns the skin. But then the cow becomes your possession; it cannot be lost, it cannot be stolen.

What is circumcision? It is branding cattle, but these cattle are Jews. Hindus have their own ways, all religions have their own ways. But it should be known whose cattle you are, who your shepherd is—Jesus? Moses? Mohammed? You are not your own master.

Those first seven years are the years when you are conditioned, stuffed with all kinds of ideas which will go on haunting you your whole life, which will go on distracting you from your potentiality, which will corrupt you, which will never allow you to see clearly. They will always come like clouds before your eyes, they will make everything confused.

Things are clear, very clear—existence is absolutely clear—but your eyes have layers upon layers of dust. And all that dust has been arranged in the first seven years of your life when you were so innocent, so trusting, that whatsoever was told to you, you accepted as truth. And whatsoever has gone into your foundation will be very difficult for you to identify later on: it has become almost part of your blood, bones, your very marrow. You will ask a thousand other questions but you will never ask about the basic foundations of your belief.

The first expression of love toward the child is to leave his first seven years absolutely innocent, unconditioned, to leave him for seven years completely wild, a pagan. Up to seven years, if a child can be left innocent, uncorrupted by the ideas of others, then to distract him from his potential growth becomes impossible. The child's first seven years are the most vulnerable. And they are in the hands of parents, teachers, priests. . . .

If you have a child, protect the child from yourself. Protect the child from others who can influence him: at least up to seven years, protect him. The child is just like a small plant, weak, soft: just a strong wind can destroy it, any animal can eat it up. You put a protective wiring around it, but that is not imprisoning, you are simply protecting. When the plant is bigger, the wires will be removed.

Protect the child from every kind of influence so that he can remain himself—and it is only a question of seven years, because then the first circle will be complete. By seven years he will be well-grounded, centered, strong enough. You don't know how strong a seven-year-old child can be because you have not seen uncorrupted children. You have seen only corrupted children; they carry the fears, the cowardliness of their fathers, mothers, their families. They are not their own selves.

If a child remains uncorrupted for seven years . . . You will be surprised to meet such a child. He will be as sharp as a sword. His eyes will be clear, his insight will be clear. And you will see a tremendous strength in him which you cannot find even in a seventy-year-old adult, because the adult's foundations are shaky. In fact as the building goes on becoming higher and higher, the more and more shaky it becomes.

If you are a parent you will need much courage, not to interfere. Open doors of unknown directions to the child so he can explore. He does not know what he has in him, nobody knows. He has to grope in the dark. Don't make him afraid of darkness, don't make him afraid of failure, don't make him afraid of the unknown. Give him support. When he is going on an unknown journey, send him with all your support, with all your love, with all your blessings. Don't let him be affected by your fears.

You may have fears, but keep them to yourself. Don't unload those fears on the child, because that will be interfering.

After seven years, the next circle of seven years, from seven to fourteen, is a new addition to life: the child's first stirring of sexual energies. But they are only a kind of rehearsal. Now when the child starts playing his sexual rehearsals, that is the time when parents interfere the most, because they have been interfered with. All that they know is what has been done to them, so they simply go on doing that to their children. Societies don't allow sexual rehearsal, at least have not allowed it up to now—only within the last two, three decades, and that too only in very advanced countries. Now children have coeducation. But in a country like India, even now coeducation starts only at the university level. The seven-year-old boy and the seven-year-old girl cannot be in the same boarding school. And this is the time for them—without any risk, without the girl getting pregnant, without any problems arising for their families—this is the time when they should be allowed all playfulness. Yes, it will have a sexual color to it, but it is rehearsal; it is not the real drama. And if you don't allow them even the rehearsal and then suddenly one day the curtain opens and the real drama starts . . . And those people don't know what is going on; even a prompter is not there to tell them what to do! You have messed up their life completely.

Those seven years, the second circle in life, is significant as a rehearsal. Boys and girls will meet, mix, play, become acquainted. And that will help humanity to drop almost 90 percent of perversions. If the children from seven to fourteen are allowed to be together, to swim together, to be naked before each other, 90 percent of perversions and 90 percent of pornography will simply disappear. Who will bother about it? When a boy has known so many girls naked, what interest can a magazine like *Playboy* have for him? When a girl has seen so many boys naked, I don't see that there is any possibility of curiosity about the other; it will simply disappear. They will grow together naturally, not as two different species of animals.

Right now that's how they grow, as if they are two different species of animals. They don't belong to one humankind; they are kept separate. A thousand and one barriers are created between them so they cannot have any rehearsal of the sexual life which is going to come.

The way children are brought up is almost butchering their whole life. Those seven years of sexual rehearsal are absolutely essential. Girls and boys should be together in schools, in hostels, in swimming pools and beds. They should rehearse for the life that is going to come; they have to get ready for it. And there is no danger, there is no problem if children are given total freedom about their growing sexual energy and are not condemned, repressed—which is being done now.

A very strange world it is in which you are living. You are born of sex, you will live for sex, your children will be born out of sex—and sex is the most condemned thing, a sin? All the religions go on putting this crap in your mind. These people all around the world are full of everything rotten that you can conceive, for the simple reason that they have not been allowed to grow in the natural way. They have not been allowed to accept themselves. They have all become ghosts. They are not authentically real people, they are only shadows of someone they could have been. They are only shadows.

The second circle of seven years is immensely important because it will prepare you for the coming seven years. If you have done the homework right, if you have played with your sexual energy just in the spirit of a sportsman—and at that time, that is the only spirit you will have—you will not become a pervert. All kinds of strange things will not come to your mind, because you are moving naturally with the other sex and the other sex is moving with you; there is no hindrance, and you are not doing anything wrong against anybody. Your conscience is clear because nobody has put into your conscience ideas of what is right, what is wrong: you are simply being whatever you are.

Then from fourteen to twenty-one your sex matures. And this is significant to understand: if the rehearsal has gone well, in the seven years when your sex matures a very strange thing happens that you may never have thought about, because you have not been given the chance. I have said to you that the second seven years, from seven to fourteen, give you a glimpse of foreplay. The third seven years give you a glimpse of afterplay. You are still together with girls or boys, but now a new phase starts in your being: you start falling in love. It is still not a biological interest. You are not interested in producing children, you are not interested in becoming husbands and wives, no. These are the years of romantic play. You are more interested in beauty, in love, in poetry, in sculpture—which are all different phases of romanticism. And unless a person has some romantic quality he will never know what afterplay is. Sex is just in the middle.

The longer the foreplay, the better the possibility of reaching the climax; the better the possibility of reaching the climax, the better opening for afterplay. And unless a couple knows afterplay they will never know what sex in its completion is.

Now there are sexologists who are teaching foreplay. A taught foreplay is not the real thing, but they are teaching it—at least they have recognized the fact that without foreplay sex cannot reach the climax. But they are at a loss how to teach afterplay because when a person has reached the climax he is no longer interested: he is finished, the job is done. For that it needs a romantic mind, a poetic mind, a mind that knows how to be thankful, how to be grateful. The person, the woman or the man who has brought you to such a climax, needs some gratitude—afterplay is your gratitude. And unless there is afterplay it simply means your sex is incomplete; and incomplete sex is the cause of all the troubles that man goes through.

Sex can become orgasmic only when afterplay and foreplay are completely balanced. Just in their balance the climax turns into orgasm.

The word "orgasm" has to be understood. It means that your whole being—body, mind, soul, everything—becomes involved, organically involved. Then it becomes a moment of meditation. To me, if your sex does not become finally a moment of meditation, you have not known what sex is. You have only heard about it, you have read about it; and the people who have been writing about it know nothing about it.

. . .

I have read hundreds of books on sexology by people who are thought to be great experts—and they are experts, but they know nothing about the innermost shrine where meditation blossoms.

Just as children are born through ordinary sex, meditation is born through extraordinary sex. Animals can produce children; there is nothing special about it. It is only man who can produce the experience of meditation as the center of orgasmic feeling. This is possible only if from fourteen to twenty-one young people are allowed to have romantic freedom.

From twenty-one to twenty-eight is the time when they can settle. They can choose a partner. And they are capable of choosing now; through all the experience of the past two circles they can choose the right partner. There is nobody else who can do it for you. It is something that is more like a hunch—not arithmetic, not astrology, not palmistry, not I-Ching, none of those things is going to help. It is a hunch: coming in contact with many, many people suddenly something clicks that had never clicked with anybody else. And it clicks with so much certainty and so absolutely that you cannot even doubt it. Even if you try to doubt it, you cannot, the certainty is so tremendous. With this click you settle.

Between twenty-one and twenty-eight somewhere, if every-thing goes smoothly the way I am saying, without interference from others, then you settle. And the most pleasant period of life comes from twenty-eight to thirty-five—the most joyous, the most peaceful and harmonious because two persons start melting and merging into each other.

What I find really amazing about your childhood is that you seem to have had an intrinsic understanding that your parents' interpretation of reality and your experience of reality were often two different things. I would be grateful for your comment.

Every child understands that he sees the world in a different way than his parents. As far as seeing is concerned, it is absolutely certain. His values are different. He may collect seashells on the beach and the parents will say, "Throw them away. Why are you wasting your time?" And for the child they were so beautiful. He can see the difference; he can see that their values are different. The parents are running after money and he wants to collect butterflies. He can't see why you are so interested in money; what are you going to do with it? The parents cannot see what the child is going to do with these butterflies or these flowers.

Every child comes to know this, that there are differences. The only question is: he is afraid to assert that he is right. As far as he is concerned, he should be left alone. It is a question of just a little courage, which is also not missing in children. But the whole society is managed in such a way that even a beautiful quality like courage in a child will be condemned.

I was not willing to bow down in the temple to a stone statue. And I said to them, "If you want, you can force me. You have more physical force than me. I am small; you can force me, but remember you are doing an ugly act. It will not be my prayer, and it will destroy even your prayer, because you are doing violence to a little child who cannot resist physically."

One day while they were inside praying in the temple, I climbed on the top of the temple, which was dangerous. Only once a year a painter used to climb it, but I had seen the painter and how he had managed. He had put nails on the back side as steps. I used those nails to climb and I was sitting on the top of the temple. When they came out they saw me sitting there and they said, "What are you doing there? In the first place, do you want to commit suicide?"

I said, "No, I simply want to make you alert that if you force me, I can do anything that is within my power. This is the answer, for you to remember that you cannot force me to do anything."

They begged me, "Be quiet. We will arrange for somebody to bring you down."

I said, "Don't be worried. If I can come up, I can come down." They had no idea about those nails. I had been particularly watching the painter, how he managed it, because everybody wondered—this painter was really great. He was painting all the temples.

I came down. They said, "We will never force you about anything, but don't do such a thing! You could have killed yourself."

I said, "The responsibility would have been on you."

It is not a question that intelligence is not in the children. It is that they just don't use their assertiveness because it is condemned by everybody. Now, everybody condemned my family because I had gone up on top of the temple—that means beyond their god, they thought it was insulting to their god.

They had a meeting of the whole family. "Leave him alone; he is really dangerous." That was the last straw! After that, they remained silent; they never told me to come to the temple, and I never went. Slowly they learned that I was not dangerous, but they should not force me into a corner.

Each child has to be assertive, that's the only thing. And what is there to lose? But children are so dependent, and I don't see that they have to be so dependent. My parents told me many times, "We will stop giving you food."

I said, "You do it. I can start begging—in this very city. I have to survive, I have to do something. You can stop giving me food, but you cannot stop me from begging. Begging is everybody's birthright."

There is not any difference of intelligence, but I see differences of assertiveness because children who are obedient are honored.

One day my father said, "You have to be back in the house before nine o'clock in the night."

I said, "If I don't come—then?"

He said, "Then the doors will not be open."

I said, "Then keep your doors closed. I will not even knock on the doors, and I am not going to come before nine. I will sit outside, and tell everybody! Whoever will be passing, they will ask, 'Why are you sitting in darkness in this cold night?' And I will tell them, 'This is the situation . . .'"

He said, "That means you will create trouble for me."

I said, "I am not creating it. You are giving this order. I have never thought about it, but when you say, 'Nine is the deadline,' then I cannot come before nine. It simply is against my intelligence. And I will not be doing anything; I will be simply sitting outside. If somebody asks, 'Why are you sitting outside . . . ?' And anybody is going to ask. If you are sitting in the road, everybody who passes by is going to ask, 'Why are you sitting here in the cold?' Then I will have to explain, 'This is the situation . . .'"

He said, "Forget about that limit. You come home whenever you want."

I said, "And I am not going to knock. The doors have to remain open. Why should the doors be closed—just to harass me? There is no reason to close the doors." In my part of India the town was always awake up to midnight, because it is so hot that only after twelve it starts cooling down. So people remain awake and work continues. The day is so hot that they may rest in the day and work in the night. I said, "There is no reason to close the doors when you are sitting inside and working. Leave the doors open. Why should I knock?"

He said, "Okay, the doors will remain open. It was my fault to say to you, 'Come inside before nine,' but it was because everybody else goes inside before nine."

I said, "I am not everybody. If it is suitable for them to come inside before nine they can come. If it is suitable for me, I will come. But don't cut my freedom, don't destroy my individuality. Just let me be myself."

It is a simple question of asserting yourself against those who have power. But you have subtle powers that you can use against them. For example, if I said, "I will simply sit in the road," I am also using power. If I am sitting on top of the temple, I am also using power. If they can threaten me, I can also threaten them. But children simply fall in line just to be respectable, just to be obedient, just to be on the right path. And the right path means whatsoever their parents are showing them.

You are right, I was a little different. But I don't think it is any superiority, just a little bit of difference. And once I learned the art, then I refined it. Once I knew how to fight with people who have power, then I refined it and managed perfectly well. I always found some way. And they were always surprised because they thought, "Now he cannot do anything against this"—because they were always thinking rationally.

I have no devotion to reason. My devotion is basically toward freedom. By what means it is achieved does not matter. Every means becomes good if it brings freedom to you, individuality to you, and you are not enslaved. The children just don't have the idea. They think that their parents are doing everything good for them.

I always made it clear to them, "I don't suspect your intentions, and I hope you don't suspect my intentions either. But there are things on which we disagree. Do you want me to agree on everything with you, whether you are right or wrong? Are you absolutely certain that you are right? If you are not so absolutely certain, then give me the freedom to decide for myself. At least I will have the pleasure of going wrong on my own decision, and I will not make you feel guilty and responsible."

One just has to be alert about one thing: whatsoever your parents say, they cannot do. They cannot harm you, they cannot kill you, they can only threaten you. Once you know they can only threaten you, their threats don't make any difference; you can also threaten them. And you can threaten them in such a way that they will have to accept your right to choose what you want to do.

So there are differences, but nothing that is special or superior. And children can be taught; they all can do the same because I have tried that too, even in my childhood. Students were puzzled: I harassed the teachers, I harassed the principal, and still they could not do anything against me. And they would do something wrong and immediately they were in trouble. They started asking me, "What is the secret?"

I said, "There is no secret. You have to be very clear that you are right and that you have a reason to support it. Then whoever is against you will see. Whether he is a teacher or the principal does not matter."

One of my teachers went in great anger into the office of the principal and fined me ten rupees for my misbehavior. I just went behind him, and while he was fining me I was standing by his side. As he moved away, with the same pen I fined him twenty rupees for his misbehavior.

He said, "What are you doing? That register is for teachers to fine the students."

I asked, "Where is it written? In this register, nowhere is it written that only teachers can fine the students. I think this register is meant to fine anybody who misbehaves. If there is anywhere else where it is written that it is only for teachers to fine the students, I would like to see it."

Meanwhile the principal came in. He said, "What is the matter?"

The teacher said, "He has spoiled the register. He has fined me twenty rupees for misbehavior."

The principal said, "That is not right."

I said, "Do you have any written document that says no student can fine a teacher, even if the teacher is misbehaving?"

The principal said, "This is a difficult matter. We don't have any document, it is just a convention that it is the teachers who punish."

I said, "It has to be changed. Punishment is perfectly okay, but it should not be one-sided. I will pay those ten rupees only if this man pays twenty rupees." Because the principal could not ask him for twenty rupees, he could not ask me for those ten rupees, and the fine is still there! When after a few years I visited the school, he showed me, "Your fine is still there."

I said, "Leave it there for other students to know."

One just has to find ways. . . !

So there must be some difference, but it is not of superiority. It is just a question of using your courage, your intelligence, and risking. What is the danger? What could those people have destroyed? At the most they could have failed me in their class—of which they were afraid, because that meant I would be again in their class the next year! So it was really favorable to me that they wanted to get rid of me as quickly as possible. That was the only power in the teacher's hands, to fail a student.

I had made it clear to every teacher, "You can fail me, it doesn't matter. Whether I pass a class in two years or three years does not matter. This whole life is so useless—somewhere I have to pass my life. I can pass my whole life in this school, but I will make your life hell because once the fear of failing disappears then I can do anything." So even the teachers who were against me were giving me better marks than needed just to help me move into another class, so I was no longer a burden to them.

If parents really love children, they will help them to be courageous—courageous even against the parents themselves. They will help them to be courageous against teachers, against society, against anybody who is going to destroy their individuality.

And that's what I mean: the new mind will have these different qualities. The children born under the new mind and the new man will not be treated the way they have been treated down the centuries. They will be encouraged to be themselves, to be assertive, to be self-respectful. And that will change the whole quality of life. It will become more shiny, alive, and more juicy.

The family has been the basic social unit for thousands of years, yet you doubt its validity. What do you suggest can replace it?

Man has outgrown the family. The utility of the family is finished; it has lived too long. It is one of the most ancient institutions so only very perceptive people can see that it is dead already. It will take time for others to recognize the fact that the family is dead.

It has done its work. It is no longer relevant in the new context of things; it is no longer relevant for the new humanity that is just being born.

The family has been good and bad. It has been a help—man has survived through it—and it has been harmful because it has corrupted the human mind. But there was no alternative in the past, there was no way to choose anything else. It was a necessary evil. That need not be so in the future. The future can have alternative styles.

My idea is that the future is not going to be one fixed pattern, it will have many alternative styles. If a few people still choose to have a family, they should have the freedom to have it. It will be a very small percentage. There are families on the earth—very rare, not more than 1 percent—which are really beautiful, which are really beneficial, in which growth happens; in which there is no authority, no power trip, no possessiveness; in which children are not destroyed, in which the wife is not trying to destroy the husband and the husband is not trying to destroy the wife; where love is and freedom exists, where people have gathered together just out of joy and not for other motives; where there is no politics. Yes, these kinds of families have existed on the earth and they are still there. For these people there is no need to change. In the future they can continue to live in families.

But for the great majority, the family is an ugly thing. You can ask the psychoanalysts and they will say that all kinds of mental disease arise out of the family. All kinds of psychoses, neuroses arise out of the family. The family creates a very, very ill human being.

There is no need; alternative styles should be possible. For me, one alternative style is the commune—it is the best. A commune means people living in a liquid family. Children belong to the commune, they belong to all. There is no personal property, no personal ego. A man lives with a woman because they feel like living together, because they cherish it, they enjoy it. The moment they feel that love is no longer happening, they don't go on clinging to each other. They say good-bye with all gratitude, with all friendship. They start moving with other people. The only problem in the past was what to do with the children. In a commune, children can belong to the commune, and that will be far better. They will have more opportunities to grow with many more kinds of people. Otherwise a child grows up with the parents and for years the mother and the father are the only two images of human beings for him. Naturally he starts imitating them. Children turn out to be imitators of their fathers and mothers, and they perpetuate the same kind of illness in the world as their parents did. They become carbon copies. It is very destructive. And there is no way for the children to do something else, they don't have any other source of information.

If a hundred people live together in a commune there will be many male members, many female members; the child need not get fixed and obsessed with one pattern of life. He can learn from his father, she can learn from her aunts and uncles, he can learn from all the men and women in the community. The child will have a bigger soul.

Families crush people and give them very small souls. In the community the child will have a bigger soul, he will have more possibilities, he will be far more enriched in his being. He will see many women; he will not have one idea of a woman. It is very destructive to have only one single idea of a woman, because throughout your whole life you will be searching and searching for your mother. Whenever you fall in love with a woman, watch! There is every possibility that you have found someone that is similar to your mother, and that may be the very thing you should have avoided.

Each child is angry with his mother. The mother has to prohibit many things, the mother has to say no—it cannot be avoided. Even a good mother sometimes has to say no, and restrict and deny. The child feels rage, anger. He hates the mother and loves the mother also, because she is his survival, his source of life and energy. So he hates the mother and loves the mother together, and that becomes the pattern. You will love a woman and you will hate the same woman, and you don't have any other kind of choice. You will always go on searching, unconsciously, for your mother. And that happens to women also, they go on searching for their fathers. Their whole life is a search to find dad as a husband. Now, your dad is not the only person in the world; the world is far richer. And in fact, if you can find the dad you will not be happy. You can be happy with a beloved, with a lover, not with your daddy. If you can find your mother you will not be happy with her. You know her already, there is nothing else to explore. That is familiar already, and familiarity breeds contempt. You should search for something new, but you don't have any image.

In a commune a child will have a richer soul. Each child will know many women, will know many men; the child will not be addicted to one or two persons.

The family creates an obsession in you, and the obsession is against humanity. If your father is fighting with somebody and you see he is wrong, that doesn't matter—you have to be with the father and on his side. Just as people say, "Wrong or right, my country is my country!" so they say, "My father is my father, wrong or right. My mother is my mother, I have to stand with her." Otherwise it will be a betrayal.

It teaches you to be unjust. You can see your mother is wrong and she is fighting with the neighbor and the neighbor is right, but you have to be with the mother. This is learning an unjust life.

In a commune you will not be attached too much to one family—there will be no family to be attached to. You will be more free, less obsessed; you will be more just. And you will have love from many sources; you will feel that life is loving. The family teaches you a kind of conflict with society, with other families. The family demands monopoly; it asks you to be for it and against all others. You have to be in the service of the family. You have to go on fighting for the name and the reputation of the family. The family teaches you ambition, conflict, aggression. In a commune you will be less aggressive, you will be more at ease with the world because you have known so many people.

That's what I am going to create here: a commune where all will be friends. Even husbands and wives should not be more than friends. Their marriage should be just an agreement between the two that they have decided to be together because they are happy together. The moment even one of them decides that unhappiness is settling, then they separate. There is no need for any divorce. Because there is no marriage, there is no divorce. One lives spontaneously.

When you live miserably, by and by you become habituated to misery. Never for a single moment should one tolerate any misery. It may have been good to live with a man in the past, and joyful, but if it is no longer joyful then you have to get out of it. There is no need to get angry and destructive, and there is no need to carry a grudge, because nothing can be done about love. Love is like a breeze. It just comes; if it is there it is there. Then it is gone, and when it is gone it is gone. Love is a mystery, you cannot manipulate it. Love should not be manipulated, love should not be legalized, love should not be forced for any reason at all.

In a commune, people will be living together just out of the sheer joy of being together, for no other reason. And when the joy has disappeared, they part. Maybe it feels sad, but they have to part. Maybe the nostalgia of the past still lingers in the mind, but they have to part. They owe it to each other that they should not live in misery, otherwise misery becomes a habit. They part with heavy hearts, but with no grudge. They will seek other partners.

In the future there will be no marriage as it has been in the past, and no divorce as it has been in the past. Life will be more liquid, more trusting. There will be more trust in the mysteries of life than in the clarities of the law, more trust in life itself than in anything— the court, the police, the priest, the church. And the children should belong to all; they should not carry the badges of their families. They will belong to the commune; the commune will take care of them.

This will be the most revolutionary step in human history—for people to start living in communes and to start being truthful, honest, trusting, and to go on dropping the law more and more.

In a family, love disappears sooner or later. In the first place it may not have been there at all, even from the very beginning. It may have been an arranged marriage—for other motives, for money, power, prestige. There may not have been any love from the very beginning. Then children are born out of a wedlock that is more like a deadlock. Children are born out of no love, and from the very beginning they become deserts. This no-love state in the house makes them dull, unloving. They learn their first lessons of life from their parents, and when the parents are unloving and there is constant jealousy and fighting and anger, all the children see is the ugly faces of their parents. Their very hope is destroyed. They can't believe that love is going to happen in their life if it has not happened in their parents' life. And they see other parents also, other families also. Children are very perceptive; they go on looking all around and observing. When they see that there is no possibility of love, they start feeling that love is only in poetry, it exists only for poets, visionaries—it has no actuality in life. And once you have learned the idea that love is just poetry, then it will never happen because you have become closed to it.

To see it happen is the only way to let it happen later on in your own life. If you see your father and mother in deep love, in great love, caring for each other, with compassion for each other, with respect for each other, then you have seen love happening. Hope arises. A seed falls into your heart and starts growing. You know it is going to happen to you, too.

If you have not seen it, how can you believe it is going to happen to you too? If it didn't happen to your parents, how can it happen to you? In fact, you will do everything to prevent it happening to you—otherwise it will look like a betrayal of your parents. This is my observation of people: women go on saying deep in the unconscious, "Look, Mom, I am suffering as much as you suffered." Boys go on saying to themselves later on, "Dad, don't be worried, my life is as miserable as yours. I have not gone beyond you, I have not betrayed you. I remain the same miserable person as you were. I carry the chain, the tradition. I am your representative, Dad, I have not betrayed you. Look, I am doing the same thing as you used to do to my mother—I am doing it to the mother of my children. And what you used to do to me, I am doing to my children. I am bringing them up in the same way you brought me up."

Each generation goes on giving its neuroses to the new people that come to the earth, and the society persists with all its madness, misery.

No, a different kind of thing is needed now. Man has come of age and the family is a thing of the past; it really has no future. The commune will be the thing that can replace the family, and it will be far more beneficial.

But in a commune only meditative people can be together. Only when you know how to celebrate life can you be together; only when you know that space I call meditation can you be together, can you be loving. The old nonsense of monopolizing love has to be dropped, then only can you live in a commune. If you go on carrying your old ideas of monopoly—that your woman should not hold somebody else's hand and your husband should not laugh with anybody else—if you carry these nonsensical things in your mind then you cannot become part of a commune.

If your husband is laughing with somebody else, it is good— your husband is laughing! Laughter is always good, with whom it happens doesn't matter. Laughter is good, laughter is a value. If your woman is holding somebody else's hand, good—warmth is flowing. The flow of warmth is good, it is a value; with whom it is happening is immaterial. And if it is happening to your woman with many people, it will go on happening with you too. If it has stopped happening with anybody else, then it is going to stop with you too. The whole old idea is so stupid!

It is as if the moment your husband goes out, you say to him, "Don't breathe anywhere else. When you come home you can breathe as much as you want, but only when you are with me can you breathe. Outside hold your breath, become a yogi. I don't want you to breathe anywhere else." Now this looks stupid. But then why should love not be like breathing? Love *is* breathing.

Breathing is the life of the body and love is the life of the soul. It is far more important than breathing. Now when your husband goes out, you make it a point that he should not laugh with anybody else, not at least with any other woman. He should not be loving to anybody else. So for twenty-three hours he is unloving, then for one hour when he is in bed with you, he pretends to love. You have killed his love, it is flowing no more. If for twenty-three hours he has to remain a yogi, holding his love, afraid, do you think he can relax suddenly for one hour? It is impossible. You destroy the man, you destroy the woman, and then you are fed up, bored. Then you start feeling, "he does not love me" and it is you who created the whole thing. Then he starts feeling that you don't love him, and you are no longer as happy as you used to be before.

When people meet on a beach, when they meet in a garden, when they are on a date, nothing is settled and everything is liquid; both are very happy. Why? Because they are free. The bird on the wing is one thing, and the same bird in a cage is another thing. They are happy because they are free.

People cannot be happy without freedom, and your old family structure destroyed freedom. And because it destroyed freedom it destroyed happiness, it destroyed love. It has been a kind of survival measure—yes, it has somehow protected the body, but it has destroyed the soul. Now there is no need for it. We have to protect the soul too. That is far more essential and far more important.

There is no future for the family, not in the sense that it has been understood up to now. There is a future for love and love rela-tionships. "Husband" and "wife" are going to become ugly and dirty words.

And whenever you monopolize the woman or the man, natu-rally you monopolize the children also. I agree totally with Thomas Gordon. He says, "I think all parents are potential child abusers, because the basic way of raising children is through power and au-thority. I think it is destructive when many parents have the idea: 'It is my kid, I can do what I want to do with my kid.'"

It is violent, it is destructive to have the idea: "It is my kid and I can do whatsoever I want with it." A child is not a thing, it is not a chair, is not a car. You cannot do whatsoever you want to do with a child. He comes through you but he does not belong to you. He belongs to existence. You are at the most a caretaker; don't become possessive.

But the whole family idea is one of possession—possess prop-erty, possess the woman, possess the man, possess children—and possessiveness is poison. Hence, I am against the family. But I am not saying that those who are really happy in their families—flowing, alive, loving—have to destroy it. No, there is no need. Their family is already a commune, a small commune.

Of course a bigger commune will be far better, with more pos-sibilities, more people. Different people bring different songs, dif-ferent people bring different lifestyles, different people bring different breaths, different breezes, different people bring different rays of light—and children should be showered with as many dif-ferent lifestyles as possible, so they can choose, so they can have the freedom to choose.

And they should be enriched by knowing so many women, so many men, that they are not obsessed by the mother's face or the father's style. Then they will be able to love many more women, many more men. Life will be more of an adventure.

Life can become a paradise here and now. The barriers have to be removed. The family is one of the greatest barriers.

ADVICE FOR PARENTS

I am concerned about my six-year-old daughter. She says she is happy but I feel that she isn't; I feel I just can't make her happy.

You seem to be too much concerned. Too much concern can be dangerous. The idea to make somebody happy never succeeds. It is against the laws of nature. When you want to make somebody happy you make him or her unhappy—because happiness is not something that can be given by somebody else. At the most you can create the situation where happiness may flower, may not flower; more cannot be done.

It seems that you are too worried about making her happy, and because you fail you become unhappy. And when you are unhappy, she will be unhappy. It is very easy to make somebody unhappy. Unhappiness is very infectious—it is like a disease. If you are unhappy, all those who are connected with you, related with you, particularly children, will become unhappy. Children are very sensitive, very fragile.

You may not say that you are unhappy but that doesn't make much difference—children are very intuitive; they have not yet lost their intuition. They still have something deeper than the intellect, which feels things immediately. Intellect takes time and intellect always wavers; it can never be certain. Even if you are unhappy and a person thinks about you, he can never be absolutely certain whether you are unhappy or you are just pretending; maybe this is just your habit or maybe your face is like that. Intellect can never come to a conclusion that is absolute.

But intuition is absolute, unconditional—it simply says what is the case. Children are intuitive and they are related in a very subtle, telepathic way. They don't look at how you look—they immediately feel. Sometimes it happens that the mother may only feel something a little later on, but the child has felt it before the mother herself. The mother may be unhappy but she is not yet aware. It is still coming to her consciousness from the unconscious—but from the unconscious to the child there is a direct passage.

To reach to your conscious it will have to pass many layers of conditioning, many layers of experiences, intellect, this and that, and it will have to pass many censors. Those censors will change the message, interpret it in different ways, color it, and by the time it reaches your conscious mind it may be absolutely something different than what it was in reality. But a child has immediate access.

Up to a certain age the children remain very much rooted in you and they know what is happening.

Just relax a little. Let her mix with other children, let her play, and don't talk about happiness, unhappiness.

Rather, you be happy. Seeing you happy, she will feel happy. Happiness is not something that we have to seek directly: it is a by-product. Children are very much puzzled when you ask, "Are you happy?" In fact they don't know how to answer it—and my feeling is that they are right! When you ask a child, "Are you happy?" she simply shrugs her shoulders . . . because what do you mean?

The child is happy only when he is not aware of it. Nobody can be happy when they are aware. Happiness is something very subtle that happens only when you are completely lost in something else.

The child is playing and she is happy, because the child does not know about herself at all in these moments—she is lost! Happiness exists only when you are lost. When you come back, happiness disappears.

A dancer is happy when the dance is there and the dancer is lost. A singer is happy when the song is so overwhelmingly there that the singer is no more. A painter is happy when he is painting. A child is happy when he is playing—maybe a nonsense game, just collecting seashells on the seashore, meaningless, but he is completely absorbed.

Have you watched a child collecting seashells or collecting stones? Just watch the absorption . . . just see how deeply involved, how utterly lost. And that is the quality of ecstasy, the quality of wonder, the quality of all religious experience. All children are religious and all children are happy unless parents make them unhappy.

But happiness is not to be sought directly. Do something else and happiness follows like a shadow—it is a consequence, not a result.

Even though I see what my parents did to me I'm still doing the same thing to my kid. So many times my own needs get in the way of what she needs. I can't seem to give her any help.

One thing to be understood is that ordinarily, whatsoever has been done by your parents becomes an engrained pattern. Whatsoever your mother did to you, that is the only way you know how to be with your child. So it is natural—nothing to be worried about—but it is good that you have become conscious of it.

Don't try to overcompensate—that's what I think you are trying to do. Now you think you are not enough—you are not giving enough love, enough care—but whatever you can give, you can give! How can you give more? Do your utmost, and if you cannot do more, don't get depressed about it; otherwise your depression will harm the child.

Now become aware, that's all. And when you start doing some old pattern, relax—don't do it!

You must have some ideal now. Your mother has not done that idealistic thing; now you have the ideal and you have to do it with the child . . . and all idealism is dangerous. So be realistic. Don't create a fiction. You must be living in a fiction. Never live with a "should." Live with the "is"—that's all there is. Whatever is, is.

Simply be yourself. Accept yourself! These shoulds are all condemnatory. This is how people move from one extreme to another.

The older generation used to think, the mothers used to think, that they were making great sacrifices for their children. They were always exhibiting that they were doing this and that. That was harmful, because love should not be a duty and it should not be talked about. You love because you feel happy. You are not doing anything to the child, you are doing something because you love to do it. The child is not obliged to you, he is not to pay you back. You love to be a mother, and you should be grateful to the child. But the older generation was not grateful to the child. They were always hoping that the child would be grateful, and when they found that the child was not grateful, they were frustrated.

Now you have moved to the other extreme.

Just be natural—these extremist points are not good. In the old times children use to be afraid of the parents; now the parents are afraid of the children—but fear remains! The wheel has moved, but it is the same fear, and a relationship can exist only when there is no fear. Love is possible only when there is no fear.

And one thing more for you, and for everybody else: the relationship between the child and the mother is such that it can never be perfect—it is impossible. Some problem will always be there. You change one problem, another will arise because the very relationship is such. Simply love the child, and leave everything else to existence. You are a human being with all the flaws and limitations of a human being, and now what can you do?

The child has chosen you to be her mother—it is not just your responsibility. The child is also responsible. There are so many women always ready to receive. She has particularly chosen you, so not only are you responsible—she is also responsible. Now just be natural and be happy! Dance with the child, love the child, hug the child. Don't carry any ideals. Don't listen to experts; these are the most mischievous people in the world, the experts. Just listen to your heart. If you feel like hugging, hug. Sometimes you feel like hitting the child, hit. And don't be worried that some great psycho-analyst says not to hit the child. Who is he to dominate you? From where does he get the authority?

Sometimes it is good to be angry. The child has to learn that his or her mother is a human being and that she can be angry too. And if you are angry, the child feels also free to be angry. If you are never angry, the child feels guilty. How to be angry with a mother who is always so sweet?

Mothers have tried to be so sweet that their whole taste is lost—they become like saccharine; they create an artificial diabetes. Don't be just sweet—sometimes bitter, sometimes sweet, as the mood arises. And let the child know that the mother has her own moods and climates—she is a human being just as the child is.

I have often been very angry with my nine-year-old son since my daughter was born. I don't love him so much.

Do one thing: whenever you feel angry with him, go into the room and instead of being angry at him, throw the anger on a pillow—beat the pillow, bite the pillow. Try it a few times and you will be surprised: It will change your relationship with the child. It is not really a question of loving or not loving. If you don't love him then it is even more essential not to be angry. If you love him, then anger can be tolerated because you compensate with love, but if you don't love him then your anger is just unforgivable. You follow me?

If one loves, then yes, anger also can be accepted because you will compensate for it: you will love him more after the anger has passed, and there will be no problem and the child will understand. But if you don't love the child and then you are angry, it is really unforgivable.

All you need is expression of anger. It accumulates in you and he has become just an excuse: you don't find anybody else there to throw it on, so you just throw on him. Children generally become scapegoats because they are helpless. You may have been angry with your husband but he was not helpless. You may have been angry with your father but he was not helpless. All that anger has accumulated; now it is channeled toward this helpless child.

So make it a point for one month: whenever you feel angry with him just leave him there, go into another room, beat the pillow, throw the pillow, bite the pillow. Within five minutes you will feel that the anger has gone and you will feel after that anger much compassion coming for the child. So just for one month try and then it will be so simple. For one month it will be an effort, because that habit will say, "Be angry at the child," and the mind will say, "This is foolish, mad, to be angry at the pillow." Once you have seen the beauty of it—that nobody is hurt, anger is released, and on the contrary you feel compassion for the child, love will arise.

And your understanding is not accurate when you say you don't love the child. If you don't love him you will not be so angry either; they go together.

Anger is nothing but love upside down, love gone sour, that's all. It has to be put right side up and it becomes love. So anger and hate are not really opposites of love. The real opposite of love is apathy, indifference. If you don't love the child you will be indifferent— who cares? And my feeling is that it has nothing to do with the child; it has something to do with your husband, with your father, with your mother.

Think of this child: he is suffering your anger for no reason at all. He cannot afford to be angry with you right now because he knows he will be defeated, he will suffer more. He will go on suppressing the anger and this anger someday or other is going to be thrown on somebody. If he can find a woman he will torture her. But if the woman is powerful, as women always are, then he will not be able to torture the wife; he will torture the son. He will have to look somewhere for some excuse, and he will have to throw it. If he cannot throw it on the child, on the wife, then on the servants or in the office—if he is a boss he will torture somebody who is just below him. And that will be unjustified, because really he wanted to torture you but that he could not do. This is how things go.

This is how from generation to generation anger passes, hatred passes, jealousy passes; all kinds of poisons go on accumulating and one generation gives it as a heritage to another generation. That's why humanity becomes more and more burdened every day. Don't do it to the child because you will spoil his whole life, and he has not done anything wrong to you.

Just try for one month and you will be surprised: this one month will change the whole pattern.

My husband and I are in conflict bringing up our son. He wants to be stricter and I want to be more loving.

So let him do his thing and you go on doing your thing; there is no problem. The child needs both, because this is how life is: if a child only gets love he will suffer; if he only gets hardness, then he will suffer. He needs both. That's the function of the mother and the father: the mother should go on giving love so the child knows that love is possible and the father remains hard so the child knows life is not so easy. It is how life is!

There are thorns and there are roses and the child has to be prepared for both. The world is not going to be a mother; the world is going to be a hard struggle. So if you just go on giving him love he will not have any bone. When life is there in reality he will simply collapse, because he will wait for the mother and she is not there; life does not bother about him. Then he will be grateful to his father because life will put him out the door many times, will shout at him, and then he will know that he can tackle that too; he has been prepared for that too.

A child has to be prepared for both softness and hardness, yin and yang both. Whatsoever the situation he will be able to respond. If life is hard, he can be hard too; if life is loving, he can be loving too; he will not have any fixation. Now if his father alone is training him he will be fixed. He will be a hard person, he will be a perfect German, but he will never be able to love and he will never be able to accept love because he does not know what love is. He will be a soldier, he will be ready to fight, to kill or be killed. That will be his only logic, he will not know anything else. That too is dangerous. That's what happened to the German nation, that's what helped Adolf Hitler. Two world wars have proved that German mothers have not been as loving as they should be and German fathers have been too disciplinarian. That's why the whole world has suffered because of Germany.

So if the child is left alone to his father, the child will become a victim of any Adolf Hitler any day; that is dangerous. If the child is left to you, the child will become too Indian, so wherever there is any fight he will simply escape, he will surrender; before even fighting he will surrender! He will be a slave. Both ways he will get stuck, fixed, and a really alive person has no fixation. He is liquid: he can move and be hard when the circumstances are such that he needs to be hard like steel, and when circumstances are such that he needs to be like a rose flower, soft and vulnerable, he can soften.

This whole expanse should be available to the child's consciousness so that he can move easily. So both are good.

***What are my responsibilities as a father? I will be separating
from my wife and we have arranged that the three boys will live
with me, while the girl will live with her mother.***

Much will have to be done because when the mother is not
there, your responsibilities become greater, bigger. You will have to
be both father and mother. But in a way it can be a great challenge
and a growth for you.

When you are just a father, your innermost core is not involved
in it, just the periphery. The father is a peripheral thing. It is insti-
tutional; it is not natural. Fathers exist only in human societies—
society has created it. It has no natural instinct; it is just a conditioning.
When a woman becomes a mother, something tremendously meaningful has happened to her. But nothing much happens to a man
who becomes a father.

For a woman it is almost a new birth. Not only the child is
born; the mother is also born. The mother gives birth to the child,
the child gives birth to the mother. When a woman gives birth to a
child, it is life. When she looks into the eyes of the child, she looks
into her own being. When the child starts growing, she grows with
the child.

So up to now you have been just a father. It was a duty, but
nothing much was involved. Now you will be both. You will have
to be both—mother also. And if you can be a mother to your children, then don't be bothered about responsibilities—they will be
fulfilled. Just start thinking in terms of being a mother. Become
more feminine, more receptive . . . . You will have to become less
and less a father, and more and more a mother. This is going to be
a great challenge and a great transformation for you.

If you can use the opportunity, you can almost achieve to a
great satori through it. Through it your inside will come to a reconciliation. The reconciliation will be within you—the man and the
woman within you, the yin and the yang within you will come to a

meeting, a crystallization. And by and by you will lose the notion of who you are—man or woman—because you will be more motherly and yet you will be a father. This can become an alchemical situation.

And my whole effort is always to give you an insight, in whatsoever situation you are in, that can become a point of growth. So just try to look at your children as if you are a mother. If you cannot do it for twenty-four hours, then at least for a few hours, and then catch hold of the man. Because it is totally different. When you are a father you would like to dominate the children. You would like to make them like you. When you are a mother you would like to give them freedom to be themselves.

You can have a certain program in your mind—that when the sun sets you will be a mother, from sunset up to sunrise. The whole day you can be a father, the whole night you can be a mother. The woman is more like the night. She surrounds you, engulfs you, drowns you, and without even touching you. When darkness surrounds you, you cannot even touch it. It is there, but it is almost as if it is not. Its very presence is through absence.

So when you are a mother become as absent as possible. Don't try to prove anything. Just be a help—and that too, very indirectly. Don't think in terms of responsibility. Think in terms of inner growth. Once you think in terms of responsibility, duty, you are already moving into anxiety. You are already losing a great opportunity. You have taken a wrong step.

Responsibility—one feels burdened. Duty—one feels one has to do it. Duty is a dirty word, a four-letter word. Love, not duty. You enjoy and you love.

And enjoy the whole situation that has happened. Then someday you may feel grateful to your wife that she left and allowed you to become a mother; otherwise it would have been impossible. And not only in this case—in every situation in life, always try to find a way how to use it for growth, how to become more yourself through it.

And meditate deeply—that will make you strong enough to face this situation and to grow from it.

My husband and I want to separate but we are worried about our daughter.

She will understand, because for her the father will remain available; there is no problem about it. So many children . . . and children are very understanding. She will feel miserable if you are miserable. But if she sees that her mother is happy, within a few days she will see that the whole thing is perfectly beautiful, nothing is wrong. You think you are miserable because of her—and she will remain miserable because of you, because the child remains in a very sympathetic relationship with the mother. If she sees that you are happy, she will forget all about it. It is not her love affair, and she has not chosen another child, adopted another child.

There is no problem—the problem is with you. Deep down you would like to see her miserable so that you can create more misery for your man: "Look what you have done to the child. You have done this to me and you have done this to the child, and you are feeling so joyful and are enjoying? We will poison your joy."

Never poison anybody's joy, because by poisoning anybody's joy you are poisoning your own well-being. Whatever you do to others will be done to you.

Just try my recipe: drop the whole thing and go dancing and say to your daughter, "This is so good—he is free, I am free, and it is perfectly beautiful."

My understanding of children is that they are so understanding. They become unnecessarily involved in the parents' fight, they are pulled in. The mother wants to pull them in, the father wants to pull them in, and the child's life becomes a misery. He becomes a politician by and by: he will say one thing to the father and something else to the mother. With the mother he will be with the mother, on her side, with the father he will be with the father. He has to become that political because he is in between these two persons. So don't create that. It is nothing. Your daughter will understand; children forget very soon.

I have problems with my two-year-old child because he is very attached to me.

Don't push him away right now, otherwise he will be negative for the whole of his life. Never push the child away. Love him as much as you can. A moment will come when he himself will start moving away from you. Then don't cling. These are natural things . . . just as when the fruit is ripe it falls from the tree automatically. When the pregnancy is nine months old, the child comes out of the womb automatically. And it is the same—whenever he grows up, he will start moving with other children. Then one day he will find a wife and will completely forget you.

So don't be worried! Just love him. And if you can love him, he will not only one day be able to forget you, he will even be able to forgive you. Right now let him cling to you. He needs your warmth, your love. Don't push him, otherwise he will stop growing. If pushed by the mother, the child feels rejected. Never reject, just allow him. It is perfectly natural. He is so helpless, that's why he clings; it is nothing like attachment. When he will be mature, strong enough, he will start moving away. Then don't try to force him not to move. Just allow him.

My daughter asks about dying. She wants to know where everything goes when it dies.

That's very good. . . . All children are interested in death; it is one of the natural curiosities. But rather than answering them, because all answers will be false . . . Never answer—just say that you don't know, that we will die and we will see. And let that be a tacit understanding about all those things for which you don't know the answers.

When a child asks anything that you don't know, accept your ignorance. Parents always think that to accept that we don't know will be harmful, our images will suffer before the child, but in fact just the opposite is the case. Sooner or later the child is going to find that you never knew and still you answered and you answered as if you knew. The day it is recognized, the child will feel that you have been cheating, and then all respect disappears. Sooner or later the child is bound to find that the parents are as ignorant as anybody else, as powerless as anybody else, as much groping in the dark as anybody else, but they pretended—and that pretension is very destructive. So whenever there is something you don't know, say, "I don't know; I'm searching and seeking."

And death is one of those things about which nothing can be said except one thing—that we go back home, we go to the same place from where we have come. We don't know, either. We come from some unknown source and we go back to that unknown source. Death is the completion of the circle, but both ends, the beginning and the end, are hidden in mystery. It is just as if a bird enters into a room from one window, flutters there for a few seconds, and escapes outside through another window. We know only when the bird is inside the room. We don't know from where it comes; we don't know where it has gone. All that we know is that small time, that interval, when the bird was inside the room.

This is the state of the whole of life. We see a child is born; the bird has entered—from where nobody knows. And then one day a person is dead; the bird has flown. Life is just between birth and death . . . a small passage.

Make the child aware of the mystery. Rather than giving the

answer it is better to make the child aware of the mysterious that's all around, so the child starts feeling more awe, more wonder. Rather than giving a flat answer, it is better to create an inquiry. Help the child to be more curious, help the child to be more inquiring. Rather than giving the answer, make the child ask more questions. If the child's heart becomes inquiring, that's enough; that's all parents can do for the child. Then the child will seek his or her own answers in his or her own way. We forget that life remains unknown—something X. We live it and yet it remains unknown. Man has progressed in knowledge; more and more is known every day; thousands of research papers go on being added to human knowledge, thousands of books go on being added. But still the fundamental remains the same. Before the fundamental we are humble and helpless.

So help her to feel the mystery more and more.

I worry about my six-year-old son. He's doing the sorts of things I don't like, like fighting and begging and lying.

Don't worry—he will not need any encounter groups later on! It is perfectly good. This is the time when they should fight and scream and say things and not be true; that will create their authenticity. These things will disappear; if they are repressed they remain. They only remain because they are repressed, otherwise when their season is past they will go.

Everybody looks childish because the childhood has not been allowed. So even a man of forty or fifty or even seventy can go into a tantrum. Just a small thing upsets him and he can become very juvenile. Just a small shock, some sadness, and he is not capable of bearing it. He has not been allowed to live his childhood; that unlived childhood goes on lingering.

Remember always, as a basic rule: we are finished with that which is lived; that which remains unlived goes on persisting, it wants to be lived. There are things that are good in childhood. The same things will be very dangerous when the childhood is gone. For example, if he screams it can be understood, if he shouts it can be understood, but when he is forty or fifty and he shouts and screams it becomes difficult to understand; then he himself feels embarrassed.

That's why so many therapy groups are growing in the world. They are needed, particularly because of Christianity. Christianity has been teaching repression, two thousand years of repression and ideas of Christian dignity. So nobody is allowed . . . Those things remain deep inside you, they wait: if some opportunity arises they will explode and if no opportunity arises, the person goes on seeking some opportunity. He may become drunk and then he will do things. He is forgiven; people say he is drunk. He can also say, "I was drunk, sorry."

People go to war, people go to see murder films. What is the joy in seeing a murder film? What is the joy in reading a detective story? It is a vicarious joy: that which you cannot do, you are doing through others, vicariously. You become identified with the murderer or the murdered, and you are thrilled. Why should people go to see a bullfight? Why should people be fighting with animals and go hunting? That seems to be so cruel and unnecessary. But there is need; something wants to be expressed, some way has to be found.

Have you not seen a football match, how a fight breaks out? The two parties and the friends of both the parties start fighting and there is chaos. Just in a football match! It is so stupid, but it goes on. That is their childhood unlived.

Allow him, don't be afraid. Your fear comes from your repression; it is not because of him. You have been repressed; you have never been allowed these things and he is being allowed. You must be feeling a little jealous deep down, and the fear is that something may go wrong. You have been taught that these things are wrong.

Just allow him. With this he will grow and he will grow beyond childhood. When he becomes mature, he will be really mature. He will never need anything like Encounter, Gestalt, Psychodrama. He has lived all that himself, and when you can really live then it goes very deep. A therapy group is a created, artificial situation; it is only a substitute, a poor substitute.

My child has some characteristics that I don't like.

If you sometimes find something in your child that you don't like, look within yourself. You will find it there; it is reflected in the child. The child is only a sensitive response. The child is simply there imbibing you, repeating you, imitating you. So if something wrong appears in the child, rather than putting it right there, put it right in yourself and you will be surprised: the child drops it automatically. The child does not only depend on the mother for physical food, he depends on her in every way—for spiritual food also. So if you become silent, the child will follow it, he will learn it unknowingly; if you become meditative, he will become meditative.

Whenever parents complain about their children, they are not aware of what they are doing, because my observation is that if something is wrong with the child, it must have come from the parents. It is almost always so: 99 percent of it comes from the parents; the smaller the child, the more is the percentage. When the child becomes a little bigger and starts moving in society, then of course he learns from others too, but in the ultimate account, almost 90 percent always comes from the parents. So whatever you want the child to become, be. Be silent, be compassionate, be loving, be joyous, and you will be surprised that just by your being that, the child starts imbibing those qualities. And this will be the greatest thing for him, if he can imbibe silence.

My little son is a very beautiful and rich child, but I feel he demands too much energy from me and needs much attention. I am in a struggle between feeling guilty and sacrificing myself. Is it possible to have a balance?

Yes, it is possible. Just one thing has to be understood. If you allow children, they can become very dictatorial; they can really exploit you. That is harmful to you and it is not good for them either, because once you allow yourself to be exploited and you have to give attention and love beyond your limits and you start feeling that this is too much, then somehow you will be taking revenge. Later on the child will grow into a world which is not going to bother about him, and he will always expect the same from everybody else. His expectations will be too much, and they will create frustrations. He will condemn you then—and it is logical too—and say, "My father destroyed me."

Give love, but don't allow yourself to be dominated. The distinction is subtle but has to be understood. Give love when you feel like giving. When you don't feel like giving, then don't be bothered, because you are not here just to fulfill your son's desires. And you are giving him a wrong example—he will do the same to his children.

And always remember—sacrifice is not good, because you will never be able to forgive the son.

But he cannot be made responsible. He is not alert, he is not so conscious. You are more conscious. Your responsibility is the greater. Give your love but don't be dominated. And children are very perceptive.

Once I was staying with a friend, and the couple went out and told me that their small son was there, so I would have to look after him. I said, "Let him play." He fell from the stairs and was hurt. He looked at me, and I sat there like a buddha. So he looked at me, watched closely, and then thought, "It is useless; to cry or to weep

is meaningless, because this man seems to be almost like a statue."
He started playing again.

Half an hour later when the parents came back, he started crying. So I said to him, "This is illogical because now there is no
problem. If there was pain or some hurt, half an hour has passed—
you should have cried before."

He said, "What was the point? I knew well that you were not
going to be bothered. I had to wait!" Children are very practical.

So from this moment become a little alert about it. For ten days,
don't allow him to force you. He will understand.

· · ·

Children can be very manipulative. They learn wrong strategies
and then they will repeat those strategies for their whole life: with
the wife, with the husband, with the children. Once you allow
them to manipulate you, next time they will do even more. They
know that you are under their power. And everybody wants to enjoy power, everybody wants to be the boss.

They can weep, they can cry. Let them cry, they have to be left
alone. And they will learn something out of it: the respect for others' freedom.

A mother is also a woman, an individual. The motherhood is
not all, it is only a part of you. That's why many women in the world,
particularly in the West, have become afraid of being mothers. The
woman has no more freedom. She is finished once she becomes a
mother, entangled, and so burdened by the problems of the children that she cannot have any space of her own. And children want
to possess; possessiveness is inborn. That disease we bring from the
very birth, to possess and grab and to hold and to cling.

Many women are afraid of becoming mothers. This is not the
way to solve the problem. The way to solve it is to see that motherhood is part of you. It is not synonymous with you; you remain an

individual. So is your being a wife just a part of you. It is not synonymous with you; you remain an individual. And the individuality
should not be sacrificed for anything, whatever it is—motherhood,
wifehood, husbandhood, fatherhood; the individuality should not
be sacrificed, because there are great implications in it.

Motherhood is not a twenty-four-hour job. Tell the children,
"When I am mothering, I am mothering, and when I am doing
something else, I am doing something else. And I don't want these
things to overlap." You will help them to become strong and to see
the point. And in their life, when they have grown up, they will feel
grateful to you and you will never feel angry. Start working along
those lines, slowly. Children are fragile but very strong too. And
they will insist, they will not easily give way because they know
you—you have been surrendering to them, so they will not easily
give way. But within two, three weeks they will understand that
this woman has changed; this woman is no longer the same.

***I am worried about the way my son doesn't eat, which may
be causing bronchitis, and about how he relates with other
children.***

What is the way? I think the problem is more with you than with
him! You seem to be too worried about him. Sometimes even that
can create tension in his mind. Take every care, but worry is not care.
Worry is very destructive. It is destructive to you, it is destructive to
him, because if he finds that you are too worried about him he will
start feeling guilty. That may cause bronchitis, that may cause
asthma. He may start eating less; he may start punishing himself.

No concern is bad, but too much concern is also bad. Extremes
are always bad; it is good to be in the middle. You are overprotect-
ing him. You can make him almost feel suffocated; that's what
bronchitis and asthma are. Asthma can start if the person feels he is
being suffocated . . . and that's what you are creating.

So your intention is not bad, but what you are doing is not good.

Just leave him on his own. Love him but leave him. He has his own life. Just give him more freedom and the asthma will disappear. Allow him his own way of life; don't try to guide him too much. All that we can do is we can love and give freedom, and love gives freedom—only then is it love.

So withdraw your concern, withdraw your worries. That may be some way of avoiding yourself. You become concerned about him so you can avoid your own worries. That becomes a good excuse, that becomes a rationalization. You can escape from your own inner chaos—you can become concerned about him. That's what millions of people are doing. Children become scapegoats. You can put all your problems on him.

If you are left alone, if there is nobody to worry about then you will have to encounter those problems. Encounter those problems; they have to be transcended.

And if you in a deep way have some investment in his being ill, in his being troubled . . . This is an investment, because if he is perfectly healthy then what will you do? You will be thrown back to yourself. So deep down somewhere in the unconscious you would like him to remain the way he is. And he will feel it; children are very intuitive. He will feel it and he will fulfill your desire. What else can he do? He will fulfill your unconscious desire and he will keep you engaged, but his life will be spoiled. And you will miss an opportunity of encountering yourself.

My feeling is that you have some deep problem to solve—that's your love. So rather than pouring everything on him, find a lover, a friend.

It happens many times that a mother can hang around the child. She can say, "What can I do? I have no time to move into any relationship—I can't afford it." No, you have to move into your own life so that you can leave him a little alone. Respect him as a grown-up. Each child has to be respected as being on the same plane.

So first: give him freedom. Don't suffocate him. That's what his asthma is saying to you; it is a message. And don't force food on him, otherwise he will reject it. There is no need! A child knows when he is hungry. When he is hungry he will eat. If he is not hungry there is no need to eat. And it is such a natural thing that no child is going to remain hungry. If someday he misses one meal, don't be worried; that's perfectly okay. Once in a while a holiday is good. Let him miss the meal. When his real hunger comes, he will come running! Many mothers force food on the child and destroy many things in doing that. Once they destroy the natural appetite of the child, by and by he becomes completely oblivious; when he is hungry, when he is not hungry, he knows not. No animal starves. When the animal is hungry he will eat; when he is not hungry he will not eat. No mother is taking care of him; nobody is guiding him. And children are animals, pure animals.

Just leave him! And within a month he will start eating in his own way. Whatever he likes, let him eat. Keep your plans and your knowledge of how a child has to be brought up to yourself, and if you have any guidebooks, burn them! Because in the West people have guidebooks. They are reading books and trying to follow what the knowledgeable people, experts, say should be done. There is no need at all—nature is enough! And give him freedom: let him move, let him do things in his own way. Within three months your problems will disappear.

But you have to tackle your own problems! When a mother becomes too much concerned about the child it means she is trying to find herself in the child, or in the child and the husband both. That's dangerous! You should start looking for a friend. That will divert your mind from him and it will save him!

I feel my young son is very strong and I don't feel strong at all. I don't know what to do in certain situations.

Let him be strong! Why should you be worried about his strength? It is good. He has to be strong and the mother has to be soft. He has to be strong; only then can he grow into an individual. If he is soft and the mother is strong, he will be killed. That's what happens to many people: the mother is too strong and they are soft, or the mother would not allow them to be strong. Then they go on hanging around the mother for their whole life. Even if they are old and the mother is dead and gone they are still holding on to her apron strings; deep down they still psychologically depend on her. That becomes pathology. Then the man may start looking at his wife as if she is his mother. He cannot live without a mother; he needs somebody to mother him.

Because of this tendency, breasts have become so important. Artists go on painting breasts, sculptors go on sculpting breasts, poets go on writing about breasts; it seems to be really a great obsession. Basically it is just an indication that these people are still hankering for the mother; the breast represents the mother. If children are free of the mother, the breast will disappear from poetry and films and painting. They will take the right proportion, they will be natural parts of the body. Right now it seems that it is not the woman who has breasts but the breasts who have the woman; the woman seems to be secondary. This is a pathological state.

Children have to be very strong, so help him to be strong. It will be difficult for you to manage because the stronger he is, the more trouble he will create for you; if he is weak, there is no trouble. But one has to be strong in life: life creates trouble, life is risky, it is challenging. If he is dull and stale and just dead, he will sit in a corner and will not give you any inconvenience but then he is not alive. If he is alive he will create many problems for you. You have to face them. That's what it means to be a mother: to face those problems. And by facing them you will also grow, by giving him freedom and strength you will also grow. Mother and child grow together.

I am concerned about screaming at my daughter. She sometimes makes me nervous and so I scream at her to stop it.

No, don't be worried about screaming—not at all. It is natural. Just one thing you have to remember—balance it by loving.

There are moments when one wants to scream—and the children understand that, because they themselves scream. That is really their language. If you are feeling boiling within and you don't scream, the child feels disturbed at what is happening, because it is beyond her to understand. She can feel it. . . . Your very vibe is screaming and you are not screaming; you are even smiling, controlling. The child is disturbed very much by that because she feels the mother is cheating—and children never forgive cheating.

They are always ready to accept truth. Children are very empirical, very down to earth.

So scream when you feel like it. The only thing to remember is to balance it by love. Then love also madly. When you are screaming at children, you have to love them also, just in the same mad way. Hug them, dance with them. They will understand that their mother is wild, and they know that she loves them so she has the right to scream also. If you only scream and don't love them with intensity and passion, then there is a problem. So the problem does not arise out of screaming. It arises if you don't balance it by love.

When a child comes and she has done something wrong, she comes ready to be beaten, slapped. If you don't slap her, her expectations are not fulfilled, she will be frustrated. If you hit her hard, nothing is wrong, only it should be warm. That hit should be warm, not cold—and there is a great difference between the two. A cold hit or a cold slapping comes only if you repress.

For example a child has done something and you have repressed your anger—this was the warm moment. If you had hit her, screamed at her, everything would have been warm and alive, but you repressed it. Later when the child is not doing anything—six hours have passed and she has forgotten completely—you cannot forget. You have repressed it; now the whole thing has gone cold. Now you find some excuse: "You have not done your homework!" Now this is cold and you are taking revenge. You have to do something, otherwise you will not be able to get rid of it. So you find some rational excuse. Screaming was very irrational, but natural. You will find some unnatural but rational excuse—that she has not done her homework or her clothes are dirty or she has not taken a shower today. Now you are angry but your anger is cold. You may get rid of it; that too will be ugly.

It is just like eating cold food—it takes longer to digest; it becomes heavy on the stomach.

The child cannot understand. So be warm. Don't listen to what psychologists go on talking about—50 percent of it is almost rubbish. They have destroyed many beautiful things in the world. Now mothers and fathers are reading their manuals on how to behave with their children. What foolishness! One simply knows . . . by being a mother you know how to behave. No need to learn from anybody. Just be natural.

No cat goes and consults any manual on how to catch rats. She simply jumps and catches. She is a cat—that's enough! No certificate is needed, no counselors are needed. You are a mother—finished! Your mother nature will take care. If you are natural it will balance itself.

Sometimes sing and dance also because you have such a beautiful child. Sometimes hug her, take her close. Let her feel your body and feel her body. She is part of your body. She needs your warmth. Sometimes take her hand and run around the house . . . go swimming.

Sometimes take her in the shower and stand naked, both stand naked under the shower, and then she'll understand perfectly well that her mother is natural; whatsoever she does is right.

My children have become unruly, unmanageable. What should I do?

Just leave them to themselves!

Simply relax. And once they see that you have relaxed utterly, and you are not worried at all what they are doing, they will become very cool and understanding themselves. The best way to control children is . . . if you can become a little chaotic, they will become controlled. Jump and dance and sing and they will start thinking, "What has happened to our mother? Is she crazy or something?" And they will start thinking, "If neighbors come to know, what will they think?" They will start controlling you and trying to hush you up!

The best way to control them is this: you do whatsoever you want to do and let them do whatsoever they want to do. And you will be surprised. Even small children—this always happens—if they see that nobody is looking after them and that they even have to look after their mother, they become very silent and disciplined. They start playing the role of the parents. Let them come to me to say, "It is becoming very difficult, how to control our mother?"

Don't be worried! They are just hippies and nothing else.

How can our child remain nonserious?

Teach her to laugh more and more. And when you play with her, keep the atmosphere of laughter around her. If you can avoid seriousness, you will be fulfilling your duty. Children are crushed under seriousness. Certainly older people are more serious and children are like laughter, but by and by they start imitating; they start feeling as if laughter is something wrong. Older people create an impression in their minds that to be serious, to keep quiet, to be silent, is something good, virtuous. That is wrong, because once the child loses contact with laughter it is very difficult to get back in contact with it. So many therapies are needed, and even then it is difficult to get your childhood back. So many religions are needed.

In fact there is no need for any religion in the world. If children are allowed to be natural, laughing, allowed fun, spontaneity, no religion is needed, no church is needed. People will be religious without any religion, and people will be religious without any church. Their whole life will be worship, because laughter is a prayer.

The moment the child loses fun, death has settled in, and near the age of three a child starts dying. That's why even in old age people remember that there was paradise in childhood—childhood was heaven. That feeling that something has been lost continues— the Garden of Eden has been lost, Adam has been expelled.

So whenever you have a child, you have a Garden of Eden around you. Don't force the child to become serious. Rather you should lose seriousness when you are with her. Laugh and become a child. If you can help that much, she will grow into a beautiful person.

Should children be told all the facts of life, irrespective of their age?

It has always been a problem down the ages—what to tell children and what not to tell. In the past the strategy was not to tell about the facts of life, to avoid it as far as possible, because people were very much afraid about the facts of life.

The very phrase "facts of life" is a euphemism; it simply hides a simple thing. Not to say anything about sex, even to avoid the word "sex" they have made this metaphor, "facts of life." What facts of life?—it is just not to say anything about sex.

The whole past of humanity has lived with that deception, but the children discover sooner or later. And in fact they discover sooner rather than later, and they discover in a very wrong way. Because no right person is ready to tell them, they have to do their work on their own. They collect, they become peeping Toms—and you are responsible for reducing them to peeping Toms. They collect from all wrong sources, from ugly people. They will carry those wrong notions their whole lives, and you are the cause of it. Their whole sex life may be affected by that wrong information that they have gathered.

Now there is as much wrong information prevalent in the world about sex as is possible. Even in this century people are living with immense ignorance about sex, even people who you would think should know better. Even your doctor does not really know what sex is, does not know its complexity. He should know, but even doctors live very superstitiously; they also know things from the marketplace. In no college is sex taught as a separate subject—such an immense, powerful subject and yet nothing is taught about it. Yes, the physiology of sex is known by the physician, but the physiology is not all; there are deeper layers: there is psychology, there is spirituality. There is a psychology to sex and there is a spirituality to sex; the physiology is only the surface. Much research has been done there, and in this century we know more than ever before, but the knowledge is not becoming prevalent.

People are afraid because their parents were afraid, and that fear has become infectious. You have to tell your children about it, you owe it to them. And you have to be truthful.

"Mom, do we get our food from God?"

"Yes, we do, Barbara."

"And at Christmastime does Santa bring all our presents?"

"That's right."

"And on my birthday the good fairy brings presents?"

"Hmm . . ."

"And did the stork bring little brother?"

"True."

"Then what the heck does Pop hang around here for?"

It is better to be truthful! But I am not saying to jump upon your children and start being truthful whether they want it or not. Now that is happening—the other extreme—because the psychologists go on saying that the truth has to be told. People go on telling the truth whether the children are inquiring about it or not. That too is wrong. Wait! If the child inquires, be truthful; if he does not inquire there is no need, he is not interested yet.

At the dinner table the old man almost choked when his little eight-year-old boy asked, "Daddy, where do I come from?"

Reddening, Pop said, "Well, I guess the time has come for you and me to have a man-to-man talk. After dinner I will tell you about the birds and the bees."

The kid said, "What birds and bees? Little Frankie down the block told me he came from Chicago. All I want to know is where I come from!"

So wait a little. They themselves will ask, you are not to be in such a hurry. And don't try in any way to deceive the children. It can be dangerous.

5

teenagers

Why is the new generation such a problem to the parents?

Because the new generation is more intelligent. Intelligence brings problems. And it is natural that the new generation should be more intelligent. That's how evolution happens. Each new generation is going to be more intelligent than the preceding one. Your children will be more intelligent than you, and your children's children will be more intelligent than your children. It is a momentum, a gathering momentum. You are standing on the shoulders of the buddhas—the whole past is yours. For example, in my being, Buddha is a part, Jesus is a part, Abraham is a part, Krishna is a part, Mohammed is a part . . . in that way Buddha was poorer than me; Jesus was poorer than me. And some future enlightened person will be richer than me because I will be part of his being, but he cannot be part of my being. Evolution goes on gathering momentum.

Each child should be more intelligent than the parents—but that brings trouble, because that is what offends the parents. Parents would like to pretend that they are all-knowing. In the past it was easy to pretend because there was no other way to impart knowledge to the children than by oral communication from the parents. For example, a carpenter's son would learn all that he would ever learn through the father. The father would not only be a father but a teacher also. And the son would always respect and be in awe of him, because the father knew so much—he knew everything about all kinds of trees and wood and this and that, and the son knew nothing. He would have tremendous respect.

Age used to be respected: the older a man was, in the ancient days, the more wise—of course, because of his experiences. But now we have invented better means of communication. The father is no longer the teacher; now the teaching profession is a totally different profession. The child goes to school, but the father had gone to school thirty or forty years before. In these thirty, forty years there has happened a knowledge explosion. The child will learn something that the father is not aware of, and when the child comes home, how can he feel any awe?—because now he knows more than the father, he is more up to date than the father. The father seems to be outmoded.

This is the problem, and it is going to be so more and more, because our expectations are old and we still want the child to respect the parents as he used to respect them in the past—but the whole situation has changed. You will have to learn something new now: start respecting the child. Now, the new has to be respected more than the old. Start learning from the child, because he knows better than you. When your son or your daughter comes home from the university, they certainly know better than you.

That has been my experience at the university. One of my philosophy professors used to talk such nonsense, and the reason was that he had been to school thirty years in the past. In those days, when he was a student, Hegel and Bradley were the most important figures in the world of philosophy. Now nobody cares about

Hegel and Bradley. Now Wittgenstein and G. E. Moore have taken their place, other philosophers have taken their place.

This professor had no idea of Wittgenstein, no idea of G. E. Moore. He was so outmoded that I had to tell him. "You are so old, so useless, that either you should start reading what is happening now in philosophy or you should stop teaching!" Naturally, he was angry—I was expelled from the university. He wrote a letter to the vice chancellor and said, "Either I am going to teach or this student is to remain in the university, but we cannot both remain together. He is trouble."

He was not ready to read Wittgenstein. In fact, I can understand his problem: even if he had read he would not have understood. Wittgenstein is a totally different world from Hegel. And he used to talk about Hume and Berkeley . . . which are rotten names, no longer of any significance—part of history, part of the footnotes.

This is the problem. Age in itself cannot now be any reason for respect. Intelligence, consciousness, they should be respected. And if you respect your children, they will respect you. But only if you respect your children will they respect you. The old way was that you go on humiliating the children, you go on insulting them in every possible way, and they have to respect you—now this cannot be the case anymore.

> The preacher's wife, while shopping, noticed a sign in the butcher's shop: Dam Ham on Sale. Slightly taken aback by such a name, she confronted the butcher about the use of profanity, but was reassured when he explained that this was a new breed of hogs being raised up by Hoover Dam, hence the name "Dam Ham." She decided to take some home and fix it for her family that evening.
>
> When her husband arrived home, she was cooking and he asked, "What's for dinner? '

"Dam ham," she replied.

The minister, who had never heard such language in his house, began to reproach her, but after she explained he felt a little embarrassed for doubting his wife.

That evening as they sat down to dinner with their six-year-old son, the minister said grace and then asked, "Pass the dam ham, please."

The little kid looked up, his eyes got big, and he said, "Now you are talking, Dad. Pass the fucking potatoes too!"

"I never slept with a man before I slept with your father," declares the stern mother to her wild daughter. "Will you be able to say the same thing to your daughter?"

"Yes," replies the girl, "but not with such a straight face!"

"Just look at me!" declares old man Rubenstein. "I don't smoke, drink, or chase women, and tomorrow I will celebrate my eightieth birthday."

"You will?" asked his son curiously. "How?"

How can teenagers create a bridge to their parents?

First, the teenagers should be honest and true, whatever the consequence. They should say to their parents whatever their feeling is—not arrogantly, but humbly. They should not hide anything from their parents. That is what is making the gap: parents are hiding many things from the children, children are hiding many things from the parents, and the gap becomes bigger and bigger.

One day I went to my father and I told him, "I want to start smoking cigarettes."

He said, "What?"

I said, "You have to give me money for it because I don't want to steal. If you don't give me I will steal, but the responsibility will be yours. If you don't allow me to smoke, I will smoke but I will smoke in hiding. You will be making me a thief; you will be making me hide things and not be honest and open. I see so many people smoking cigarettes that I want to taste. I want the best cigarettes available, and I will smoke the first cigarette in front of you."

He said, "This is strange, but your argument is right. If I prevent it, you will steal. If I prevent it you will still smoke, so my preventing you will create more criminal things in you. It hurts me. I don't want you to start smoking."

I said, "That is not the question. The desire has arisen in me, seeing people smoking. I want to check whether it is worth it. If it is worth it, then you will have to supply me with cigarettes. If it is not worth it, then I am finished with it. But I don't want to do anything until you refuse; then the whole responsibility is yours, because I don't want to feel guilty."

He had to purchase the best cigarettes possible in the town—reluctantly. My uncles, my grandfather, were saying, "What are you doing? This is not done." They were adamant about it. But my father said, "I know this is not done, but you don't know him as well as I know him. He will do exactly what he is saying, and I respect his truthfulness, his honesty. He has made his plan completely clear to me: 'Don't force me and don't prevent me, because that will make me feel guilty.'"

I smoked the cigarette, coughed, tears came to my eyes; I could not even finish one cigarette, and I dropped it. I told my father, "This is finished. You need not worry now. But I want you to understand that I will tell you about anything I feel so that there is no need to hide anything from you. And if I hide even from my father then who am I going to relate with? No, I don't want to create any gap between me and you."

Seeing that I dropped the cigarettes, tears came to his eyes. He said, "Everybody was against it, but your sincerity forced me to bring the cigarettes." Otherwise, in India perhaps no father has ever offered cigarettes to the son; it is unheard of. Fathers don't even smoke in front of their sons so that the very idea of smoking does not arise.

Teenagers are in a very difficult situation. They are changing; they are leaving childhood behind and they are becoming youngsters. Every day new dimensions of life are opening for them. They are in a transformation. They need immense help from the parents. But right now the situation is that they don't meet the parents at all. They live in the same house but they don't talk with each other because they cannot understand each other's language, they cannot understand each other's viewpoints. They meet only when the boy or the girl needs money; otherwise there is no meeting. The gap goes on becoming bigger; they become as much strangers as one can imagine. This is really a calamity.

Teenagers should be encouraged to say everything to their parents without any fear. This is not only going to help the children, it is going to help the parents too.

Truth has a beauty of its own; honesty has a beauty of its own. When teenagers approach their parents with honesty, truth, sincerity, and just open their hearts, it triggers something in the parents to open their hearts also, because they are also burdened with many things which they want to say but cannot. The society prohibits, the religion prohibits, the tradition prohibits. But if they see the teenagers being completely open and clean it will help them also to be open and clean. And the so-called, much-discussed generation gap can simply be dropped; it can evaporate on its own accord.

The most troublesome problem is about sex. The children should be able to say exactly what is going on in their minds; there is no need to hide anything, because whatsoever is going on in their minds is natural. They should ask the advice of the parents—What can be done?—they are in a troubled state, and they need help. And to whom can they go except their parents?

If any problem was there, I simply told my parents. And that's my suggestion: the teenagers should not hide anything from the parents, from the teachers . . . they should be absolutely sincere, and the gap will evaporate. And we need the gap to evaporate, because what kind of society is this? There is a gap between parents and children, there is a gap between husband and wife, there is a gap between teachers and the taught. There are only gaps and gaps all around.

Everybody is surrounded with all kinds of gaps as if all communication has broken down. This is not a society, this is not a commune—because there is no communication. Nobody can say the right thing, everybody is repressed. Everybody is suppressing his desires, and everybody is angry, and everybody is feeling lonely, frustrated. We have created an angry generation; we have created philosophies of meaninglessness. And the whole reason for all this is that children have lost contact with the parents. Children can do a tremendous job, and they have the courage to do it. Perhaps parents may not be able to do it; they are much too conditioned. The teenagers are young and fresh; just teach them to be sincere with their parents.

I made a contract with my father. I told him, "I want to make a contract."

He said, "About what?"

I said, "The contract is that if I say the truth you have to reward me, not to punish me. Because if you punish me, then next time I will not say the truth."

And that's how it is happening all over the world: truth is being punished, so then the person stops saying it. Then he starts lying because lying is rewarded.

So I said to him, "You can decide. If you want me to lie, I can lie . . . if that is what you are going to reward. But if you are ready to reward the truth, then I will say the truth—but you cannot punish me for it."

He said, "I accept the contract." It is a simple method. If you cannot expose yourself to your own father and mother . . . in this whole world everybody is more of a stranger than them. Your father and mother are also strangers, but they are the closest strangers, the most intimate strangers. Expose yourself to them so no gap exists. This will help them also to be sincere with you. This is something to be remembered: that sincerity, honesty, truth, trigger in the other person also the same qualities.

At this young age there is a lot of shyness and insecurity about making decisions. Parents are not often helpful. How to develop the inner strength?

All shyness is basically concerned with sex. Once children are perfectly free to have sexual relationships, you will see a tremendous change. They are no longer shy; they become, for the first time, decisive without any training for decisiveness because a great biological burden has been removed from them, a great psychological tension has relaxed.

I don't see that there is any need to teach children how to be decisive. All that is needed is to give them freedom as far as love is concerned. And now that the pill is available, there is no fear of any girl getting pregnant; it is simple, a game, a playfulness. This will bring a certain strength in boys and girls which you cannot conceive was connected with their sexuality.

People are nervous about sex if they are repressed; if they have repressed sexuality they are hesitant about everything. They don't know what is right and what is wrong, what to do and what not to do, because about a very basic thing they are not allowed to make a decision, which is fundamental because it concerns life itself.

My understanding is that once children are given freedom about sex, and sex is accepted as a very normal thing—that's what it is—they will come out with great decisiveness about other things, because for the first time they will not be repressed. It is repression that creates all kinds of troubles, shyness, indecisiveness . . . because deep inside they are continuously fighting with their own nature.

When there is no inner fight and no inner split—they are one solid individual—you will see a totally new kind of child in front of you with strength, decisiveness, with no shyness.

So this question can be solved if the first question is solved without any trouble.

Teenagers have a strong desire to belong to a group, to anything. What does this need reflect?

It is just because they don't belong to the family anymore, and they are too young and too afraid to be alone in the world. If there were not this gap between them and their parents, there would have been no need of any such groups. There are still places in the East where you don't see this kind of thing happening—hippies or punks or skinheads. You don't see such a thing happening at all for the simple reason that children belong to the family. They have roots in the family, they are not alone; there is not such a gap as exists in the West.

This gap is creating the whole problem. Then the teenagers want to belong to *any* group because they feel afraid to be alone. They are too young, too vulnerable, so they start belonging to any group that is available in the vicinity. And anybody can exploit them. They can be forced to do crime—they *are* doing crime—they can be forced into drugs, selling drugs, and they *are* doing it. And some cunning people can manage those groups and exploit the young people, all for their need to belong. For that also, first, the gap should be dropped.

Secondly, you should create some other groups. In the whole of history there have been many. For example, there were people who belonged to Socrates's school, young people in search of truth. Everybody in Athens who had some intelligence moved into Socrates's influence. And he was not alone: all over the East there were many sophists whose whole work was to teach people how to argue. Thousands of young people belonged to those sophist schools just to learn argument, very refined argument.

In India we had many schools—different philosophers proposing different philosophies—and young people were interested. Old people had already settled down; the young people were the moving generations. Nobody was preventing them; they could go to any teacher. They could change their teachers, they could learn so much, and from original thinkers—not like the dull and dead universities of today where you find only professors who are just parrots and have nothing of the original.

Each original thinker was a university in himself, and thousands of disciples around him were learning about everything in life from a certain angle—and not only learning it but living it, experiencing it before they settled into life. So rather than becoming skinheads they were with Nagarjuna, or with Basho, or with Chuang Tzu, or with Pythagoras, or with Heraclitus, or with Epicurus. And that was something beautiful.

Young people have come to me, and a great family has arisen around the world. There is a certain belonging, very loose, so nobody is in a slavery; everybody is free and yet he feels some kind of synchronicity with thousands of people.

I can change all those terrorists, all those skinheads without any difficulty. I have changed many hippies; now you cannot recognize them. Even they may have forgotten that the first time when they came to me . . .

We need more wandering philosophers around the world,

wandering teachers around the world so that young people can belong to them and learn something—and live something.

Teenagers often have fantasies and dreams regarding their future. How can they be more realistic?

They need not be. There is a time for fantasy, dreams, and it is good for teenagers to have fantasies and dreams rather than making them realistic. That means you are destroying their youthfulness and you are making them adult before their time.

No, those dreams and fantasies are part of growth; they will disappear by themselves. Life itself will make them realistic; before they enter life, let them enjoy their dreams—because in life there are only nightmares, only miseries and sufferings. They will become very realistic, but they will always remember those days of dreams and fantasies as the most beautiful. What can your reality provide in place of dreams and fantasies?

Unless you are ready for teenagers to move into meditations . . . that will not make them realistic, that will make them utopians. That will make them far more difficult to be adjusted in your rotten society than the dreams and the fantasies.

These dreams and fantasies can do no harm. They are part of life; that's how youth has always dreamt, fantasized.

Let them dream and fantasize, they are not harming you. And soon they will be burdened with duties, jobs, children, wives. Before that they have a little time; let them use it in fantasy, there is no harm.

As far as I am concerned, my feeling is that their experience of this dream time will help them to remember that life can be different; it need not be miserable, it need not be a suffering. It is not necessarily a misery.

They have lived beautifully—and those were only dreams. There is a possibility to have a conscious transformation in which you can have far more beautiful experiences than any dreams can give you. But the taste of dreams is good; it will keep you alert that misery is not all. Something else is possible.

Youth is the time for dreams and hopes, and when you are lost into the so-called real world those moments will remind you, "Is there some way to really find a state of being, of peace, serenity, silence, and joy?"

So I don't think there is any need to change it.

Can you please talk about youth and sports, which today has a strong impact on young people's lives.

It is a great relief that it is the last question, because these teenagers can go on asking!

Sports are perfectly right, and the teenagers should be encouraged not just to be observers of other people playing, but to be participants. What is happening is that thousands of people are just watching, and only a few people, professionals, are playing. This is not a good situation. Every teenager should be a participant, because it is going to give him physical health, it is going to give him a certain agility, it is going to give him a certain intelligence, and it is perfectly youthful.

But just to be an observer—and to be that in front of a television set—is not right. Five or six hours glued in your chair in front of a television set just seeing others playing football, or any other sport, is not right. It does not give you any growth. On the contrary, it makes you only an outsider in everything, never a participant, when it is deeply needed to be a participant, involved, committed.

It is good once in a while to see experts playing, to learn—but just to learn; otherwise everybody should be on the playgrounds. I don't see what the problem is. Young people should play; even elderly people, if they can find time, should play. Even people who have retired, who want to live a little more, should play. We should find games for every age group so that all people, their whole life, are players—according to their age, according to their strength.

But life should be a sport.

Sport has one very beautiful thing which I would like you to remember: it teaches you that it does not matter whether you are defeated or you are victorious. What matters is that you play well, that you play totally, that you play intensely, that you put your all into it without holding back. That is sportsmanship. The others can be victorious, there is no jealousy; you can congratulate them and you can celebrate their victory. All that is needed is that you are not holding back, you are putting all your energies into it.

Your whole life should be a playfulness.

So there is nothing wrong in teenagers being interested in sports. The person who is asking seems to be interested that they should be all in the schools learning geography, history, and all kinds of nonsense which is of no use in life. Sports are far more significant, far healthier, far livelier.

Many young people choose to look ugly. They dress up as punks or skinheads, shaving part of their hair and dyeing the rest in outrageous colors. They also prefer to wear ragged clothing. Can you please comment on this strange phenomenon?

It is not strange at all. It is a commentary on you. They are bored with your lifestyle. They are simply showing their resentment. They are showing that you have led society not toward truth, not toward tranquility, not toward godliness; you have led society toward death. The punks and the skinheads are simply reminders that you have failed. Western civilization has come to its end. Naturally, it is always the youth who are most vulnerable to what is coming, are more perceptive. They can see that death is coming, that all the scientists, politicians, churches, are preparing a big graveyard for the whole of humanity. By their outrageous clothing, their ragged clothes, cutting half of their hair, they are simply indicating that there is still time to drop the behavior that you have been following up to now.

Nothing like this has ever happened in the East, for the simple reason that the East has been searching for something higher— higher than man. The Eastern genius has been trying to reach to the stars, and the Western genius is simply preparing for death.

These punks and these skinheads are just trying to say something to you; they are symbolic. They know you are deaf and you will not listen. Something drastic has to be done so that you start thinking, "What has gone wrong? Why are our children behaving in this way?"

What do you want?—you are preparing for nuclear warfare; you are preparing for the death of all life on this earth. Those people are not strange phenomena: *you* are a strange phenomenon! They are simply revolting against you, and it will be good to listen to them. And it will be good to change the way the West has followed up to now, the way of materialism. I am not against materialism, but materialism alone can lead only to death, because matter is dead. I am absolutely in favor of materialism if it serves spiritual needs. If materialism is a servant, and not the master, then it is perfectly good. It can do miracles to help humanity, to raise it in consciousness, in rejoicing, to raise humanity beyond humanity.

You are proving Charles Darwin wrong—because monkeys were more intelligent than you. At least they went beyond themselves and created humanity. What have you created? Go beyond yourself and create buddhas; only then will Charles Darwin be right and the theory of evolution will be true.

Man is simply stuck, and the youth are simply showing you— and they have to be outrageous because you are not going to listen to logic, to reason, to intelligence.

I am in all sympathy for those people; I would like to meet

them. I will have immediate rapport with them because I can understand their misery, their anguish. They may prove your saviors. Don't laugh at them; laugh at yourself. They are your children; you have produced them—you must take the responsibility.

A father is known by his children, just as a tree is known by its fruits. If the fruits turn out to be poisonous, then are you going to condemn the fruits or condemn the tree? You are the tree—and those insane looking young people are the fruits. Somewhere you are responsible. They are a question mark on you. Think about them sympathetically.

My own understanding is that the West has come to an end. Unless a tremendous movement of spirituality spreads over the Western world, there is no way to save it—and that's what I am trying to do. My sannyasins are also young; if they were not sannyasins, perhaps they would have been punks, they would have been skinheads. But they have found a way to live on higher levels of being. They are also in revolt; but their revolt is not reaction, their revolt is revolution. They are trying to live a life of peace, love, silence, light.

They have chosen a new way of life.

Unless you understand that the West is in urgent need of a new way of life, more and more outrageous reactions will be there around you, and you will be responsible for it.

The young generation is using all kinds of happifiers to make life worth living. Can you talk about our natural capacity to feel ecstasy.

Ecstasy is a language that man has completely forgotten. He has been forced to forget it; he has been compelled to forget it. The society is against it, the civilization is against it. The society has a tremendous investment in misery. It depends on misery, it feeds on misery, it survives on misery. The society is not for human beings.

The society is using human beings as a means for itself. The society has become more important than humanity. The culture, the civilization, the church, they all have become more important. They were meant to be for man, but now they are not for man. They have almost reversed the whole process; now man exists for them.

Every child is born ecstatic. Ecstasy is natural. It is not something that happens only to great sages. It is something that everybody brings with him into the world; everybody comes with it. It is life's innermost core. It is part of being alive. Life is ecstasy. Every child brings it into the world, but then the society jumps on the child, starts destroying the possibility of ecstasy, starts making the child miserable, starts conditioning the child.

The society is neurotic, and it cannot allow ecstatic people to be here. They are dangerous for it. Try to understand the mechanism; then things will be easier.

You cannot control an ecstatic man; it is impossible. You can only control a miserable man. An ecstatic man is bound to be free. Ecstasy is freedom. You cannot destroy him so easily; you cannot persuade him to live in a prison. He would like to dance under the stars and he would like to walk with the wind and he would like to talk with the sun and the moon. He will need the vast, the infinite, the huge, the enormous. He cannot be seduced into living in a dark cell. You cannot make a slave out of him. He will live his own life and he will do his thing. This is very difficult for the society. If there are many ecstatic people, the society will feel it is falling apart, its structure will not hold anymore.

So from the very childhood the child is not allowed to taste freedom, because once he knows what freedom is, then he will not concede, he will not compromise. He will be assertive. Once the child knows the taste of freedom, he will never become part of any society, any church, any club, any political party. He will remain an individual, he will remain free and he will create pulsations of freedom around him. His very being will become a door to freedom.

What is ecstasy? Something to be achieved? No. Something that you have to earn? No. Something that you have to become? No. Ecstasy is being, and becoming is misery. If you want to *become* something you will be miserable. Becoming is the very root cause of misery. If you want to be ecstatic—then it is just now, here-now, this very moment. Look at me. This very moment— nobody is barring the path—you can be happy. Happiness is so obvious and so easy. It is your nature. You are already carrying it. Just give it a chance to flower, to bloom.

Ecstasy is not of the head, remember. Ecstasy is of the heart. Ecstasy is not of thought; it is of feeling. And you have been deprived of feeling. You have been cut away from feeling. You don't know what feeling is. Even when you say, "I feel," you only think you feel. When you say, "I am feeling happy," watch, analyze, and you will find you *think* you are feeling happy. Even feeling has to pass through thinking. It has to pass through the censor of thinking; only when thinking approves of it is it allowed. If thinking does not approve of it, it is thrown into the unconscious, into the basement of your being, and forgotten.

Become more of the heart, less of the head. The head is just a part; the heart is your whole being. Heart is your totality. So whenever you are total in anything, you function from feeling. Whenever you are partial in anything, you function from the head.

Whenever you are totally into something, you are ecstatic. Ecstasy is of the heart, is of the total.

Why do people take drugs?

The drugs are as old as humanity itself, and they certainly fulfill something of immense value. I am against drugs, but my being against drugs is for the same reason as for thousands of years people have been addicted to the drugs. It may look very strange. The drugs are capable to give you a hallucinatory experience beyond the mundane world. That is the experience that is being searched through meditation.

Meditation brings you to the real experience, and a drug gives you just a hallucination, a dreamlike experience, but very similar. To meditate is difficult. The drug is cheap. But the attraction for drugs is spiritual.

Man is not satisfied with his mundane existence. He wants to know something more. He wants to be something more. Just the ordinary life seems so flat, so meaningless, that if this is all then suicide seems to be the only way out of it. It gives no ecstasy, no joy. On the contrary, it goes on piling you up with more and more misery, anxiety, disease, old age, and finally, death.

This is the reason that drugs have attracted man since the very beginning. And they have at least given him a temporary relief. Only a few people tried meditation. Under proper guidance—medical, meditational—drugs can be of immense help. I said I am against drugs because if they become addictive then they will be the most destructive for your journey toward the self. Then you become enchanted into hallucinations. And because it is cheap—no effort has to be done, just you have to go on taking bigger and bigger doses. . . .

For thousands of years people have been using drugs. Moralists, religious people, governments have been trying prohibition absolutely unsuccessfully. And I don't see that they can ever succeed. The only way to succeed is what I am suggesting. Rather than prohibiting drugs, let the scientists find better drugs that give deeper and more psychedelic, more colorful, more ecstatic experiences and without any side effects, and without any addiction. And these should be available in the universities, in the colleges, in the hospitals—wherever some kind of guidance is possible, that the person is not prohibited, is allowed total freedom to use anything that he wants. And we use his experience to help him grow toward some authentic process so that he can start experiencing something far greater than any drug can give.

Only then can a person compare and see that the first experience was just a dream, and this experience is a reality. The first one was just cheating myself through chemistry, "and the first one was not helping me in my spiritual growth. It was in fact preventing the growth, keeping me addicted and retarded." The second one goes on growing, and now the person starts gathering courage to explore more because before, he had never been aware that these experiences are possible, that these experiences are not just fiction.

So this paranoia about drugs is not helpful to humanity. You can make drugs illegal, it makes no change. In fact, they become more attractive, more exciting. Particularly to the youth, they become a challenge.

I am amazed sometimes: Is man ever going to learn even the ABC of human psychology? The same stupidity of prohibition goes on happening that God did with Adam and Eve. "Don't eat the fruit of this tree." But that becomes an invitation, that becomes a challenge.

Thousands of years have passed, but the authority figures are still in the same mood: "Don't use the drug, otherwise imprisonment for five years, seven years." And nobody bothers that drugs are being made available in jails. Just you have to pay a little higher price. And the people who come out of the jail are not cured. They go back again because the drug gives them something your society is not giving them. They are ready to destroy their health, their body, their whole life becomes a mess, but still that drug gives them something that your society does not give.

So rather than preventing them, create a society that gives something better. Your life gives them nothing. You suck them of their blood and in return, what do they get? No joy, just anxieties upon anxieties. Or sometimes alcohol makes them relax for a few hours, sing a song or have a little dance—or a fight in the pub. But for a few hours they are transported from your world. The very attraction proves that your society is wrong, not that alcohol is wrong.

Your society should help people to dance, to sing, to rejoice, to love.

I am against drugs because they can become addictive and they can prevent your spiritual growth. You can start thinking that you have achieved what you were seeking, but your hands are empty. You are just dreaming.

But, on the other hand, I have a very scientific mind. On the other hand I would like drugs to be used, not to be prohibited—but used under proper guidance as a stepping-stone toward meditation.

Governments should pay more attention to improving the drugs rather than preventing people. If improved drugs are available, then other drugs will already be out of the market. There is no need to prohibit anything in the world. Just produce something better— something better, cheaper, legal. Then who is going to bother about marijuana, hashish, heroin—for what? There is no reason. Something better is available with the medical store, without prescription. Even in the hospital you can book a place for yourself, so that doctors can look after you while you are in the drug experience. Meditators can help you to understand what has happened to you. And this is possible very easily through meditation.

Just one or two sessions with a guide will be enough. The person can be moved toward meditation. And once a person moves toward meditation, drugs have no importance at all.

All the efforts of scientists and the government should be to understand that if a certain thing has been so attractive for the whole history of man, and no government has ever been successful to prohibit it, then there must be a certain need that it fulfills. Unless that need is fulfilled in some other way, drugs are going to remain in the world.

They are destructive. And the more governments are against them, the more destructive they are, because nobody can make any refinements of them, nobody can make any experiments with them; nobody is even allowed to say what I am saying. But I can say it because I am against drugs. But that does not mean they cannot be used. They can be used as a means, they are not the end.

If we can hope a future free of drugs, if people become naturally meditative. . . . And that is possible. If a child finds his father is meditating, his mother is meditating, everybody is meditating, he will start being curious about it. He also wants to meditate. And that is the age when meditation is very simple because the child is not yet corrupted by the society. The child is still innocent. And if everybody around him is doing something and enjoying in doing it, he cannot remain behind. He will sit with them with closed eyes. First they may laugh at him, thinking it is not possible for children to meditate. But they do not understand. It is more possible for children than for the so-called grown-ups.

Just the atmosphere of meditation in schools, in colleges, in universities—wherever the person goes he finds that atmosphere which nourishes his own meditativeness. I would love to see that no drugs are needed in the world. But not through prohibition, through creating something better, something real. Drugs will be defeated in that way without any difficulty. But these idiotic governments go on giving importance to drugs and they go on destroying the youth around the world.

The most precious time of life is wasted in hallucinations, and by the time they realize what they have done to themselves, perhaps it is too late. They cannot come back to a normal state. The body has become accustomed to have certain chemicals in it. Then, even unwillingly, they have to go on injecting themselves with all kinds of poisons. Or if somebody has not been on hard drugs, and returns back to life without drugs, then he finds life very dull, more dull than you find it because he has seen something beautiful. It always remains a comparison. He has made love under the impact of a drug and felt at the very top of the world. Now he makes love and finds that it is nothing but a kind of sneeze. It feels good; you sneeze and it feels good, but it is not something that you live for. Nobody can say, "I am living here for sneezing."

My whole effort is to bring something greater than drugs can bring, and that is the decisive factor. If something can happen through meditation that gives you a better glimpse, at no cost . . . You are not paying for it with your health, your chemistry, by destroying your body and other things. You don't have to pay anything for it and it happens! You are the master of it—you are not dependent on anything for it. You can make it available any moment you want. Once you know the key, you can unlock the door whenever you want. Something greater, higher, has to be made available to you.

All over the world that has been the problem down the ages: people have tried to help others to come out of their drug trips but it almost always fails because you can't provide anything better. The people also want to get out of it—everybody wants to get out of it because it is a bondage and everybody understands that he is creating a subtle bondage that will become bigger and bigger and one day he will be surrounded by walls, China walls, and it will be difficult to get out of them. By one's own effort, one is creating such a big wall and then it will be difficult to destroy it; one will be caught in it. One's whole life will become a kind of sickness.

And it is vicious. If you take a drug, while you are under its impact everything seems good. Then out of it everything feels so dull, so meaningless that the drug seems to be the only possibility, again and again. Then the quantity of drug has to be increased and by and by one is lost. Drugs are so powerful that they destroy the very chemistry of your brain. The brain is very delicate; it cannot live with such violent coercions being done to it. Those very minute and subtle nerves start getting damaged. Then one loses alertness, intelligence, becomes dull, becomes insensitive. Then the drug remains the only possibility, the only meaning that one can get.

But just to say these things doesn't help. Just to preach doesn't help. Just to say that this is bad and a sin does not help; in fact, it makes the problem worse! The person is already in suffering and now you bring in another problem—that this is sin—so then he feels guilty, too. The drug was enough to destroy him; now guilt will destroy him also. You have added more poison to the problem. You make the person feel immoral, criminal—and these are all wrong attitudes.

The person needs help, the person needs sympathy, the person needs love. Maybe the person has missed love, hence he has moved in that direction. Maybe the society has not given what was needed, the parents have not given what was needed. So the person has become distracted. The person needs all your attention, love, care—but even that will not help unless the person comes to know and feel something that is bigger and greater than any drug can make available.

Why are we afraid and sometimes even resent taking responsibility for ourselves?

It is because from your very childhood you have been taught not to be responsible. You have been taught to depend. You have been taught to be responsible to your father, to your mother, to your family, to your motherland, to all kinds of nonsense. But you have not been told that you have to be responsible for yourself, that there is nobody who is going to take your responsibility.

On the contrary, your parents were taking your responsibility. Your family was taking your responsibility. The priest was taking your responsibility for your spiritual growth. You were just to follow all these people and do whatsoever they said. When you are grown up and you are no longer a child, a great fear arises because you have to take responsibility and you have not been trained for it.

You go to confess your sin to the priest . . . what kind of stupidity are you doing? First, to think that you have committed sin; second, feeling guilty that you have committed it; third, now you have to go to the priest to confess it, so that he can pray to God to forgive you? A simple thing has become so complex, so unnecessarily long and circuitous. Whatever you have done, you *wanted* to do it—that's why you have done it. And who is there to decide what is sin and what is not sin? There is no criterion anywhere, no weighing scale for the sin that you have committed—one kilo, two kilos, three kilos? How long a sin have you committed?—one yard, two yards, three yards? What was this sin, and who is this priest you are going to confess to?

I teach you not to be responsible to anyone: the father, the mother, the country, the religion, the party line, don't be responsible to anybody. You are not. Just be responsible for yourself. Do whatever you feel like doing: if it is wrong, the punishment will immediately follow! If it is right, the reward will follow immediately, instantly. There is no other way.

This way you start finding what is wrong, what is right, on your own. You will grow a new sensitivity. You will start seeing with a new vision. Instantly you will know what is wrong because in the past, so many times you have done it and always suffered as a consequence. You will know what is right, because whenever you did right existence showered great blessings on you. Cause and effect are together, they are not separated by years and lives.

You are responsible then. If you want and enjoy a certain act, although it brings suffering, then do it. It is good because you enjoy it. The suffering is not great enough to deter you from the enjoyment that your act brings. But it is up to you, wholly and solely up to you to decide. If the suffering is too much and the act brings nothing, no joy, and necessarily a long anguish follows it, then it is up to you—if you are an absolute idiot, what can anybody else do about it?

This is what I mean by being responsible to yourself. There is nobody on whom you can dump your responsibility, but you are always searching to dump it on somebody, even on a poor man like me, who is continually telling you that I am not responsible for anything or for anybody. Still, somehow, deep down you go on carrying the illusion that I must be joking.

I am not joking. "He is our master," you must be thinking, "how can he say that he is not responsible?" But you don't understand. Dumping your responsibility on me, you will remain retarded, childish. You will never grow. The only way to grow is to accept all good, all bad, the joyful, the sorrowful. Everything that happens to you, you are responsible for. That gives you great freedom.

Rejoice in this freedom. Rejoice in this great understanding that you are responsible for everything in your life. This will make you what I call the individual.

6

---

education

What is learning?

Learning is not knowledge. Learning has become too much identified with knowledge—it is just the opposite of knowledge. The more knowledgeable a person is, the less he is capable of learning. Hence children are more capable of learning than grown-ups. And if the grown-ups also want to remain learners, they have to go on forgetting whatsoever they have learned. Whatsoever has become knowledge in them, they have to go on dying to it. If you collect your knowledge, your inner space becomes too heavy with the past. You accumulate too much garbage.

Learning happens only when there is spaciousness. The child has that spaciousness, innocence. The beauty of the child is that he functions from the state of not-knowing. That is the fundamental secret of learning: functioning from the state of not-knowing. Watch, see, observe, but never form a conclusion. If you have already arrived at a conclusion, learning stops. If you already know, what is there to learn?

Never function from the ready-made answer that you have arrived at from the scriptures, universities, teachers, parents, or maybe your own experience. All that you have known has to be discarded in favor of learning. Then you will go on growing; then there is no end to growth. Then a person remains childlike, innocent, full of wonder and awe to the very end. Even when he is dying he continues learning. He learns life, he learns death. And the person who has learned life and learned death goes beyond both; he moves to the transcendental.

Learning is receptivity, learning is vulnerability. Learning is openness, open-endedness.

. . .

Man is born as a seed. He is born as a potentiality, he is not born as an actuality. And this is very special, this is extraordinary, because in the whole of existence only the human being is born as a potentiality; every other animal is born actual. A dog is born as a dog, he will remain the same his whole life. The lion is born as a lion. Man is not born as a human being, man is born only as a seed: he may flower, he may not. Man has a future; no other animal has a future. All animals are born instinctively perfect. Man is the only imperfect animal; hence growth, evolution, is possible.

Education is a bridge between the potentiality and the actuality. Education is to help you to become that which you are only in a seed form. And this is what I am doing here; this is a place of education. The thing that is being done in the ordinary schools and colleges and universities is not education. It only prepares you to get a good job, a good earning; it is not real education. It does not give you life. Maybe it can give you a better standard of living, but the better standard of living is not a better standard of life; they are not synonymous.

The so-called education that goes on in the world prepares you only to earn bread. And Jesus says, "Man cannot live by bread alone." And that's what your universities have been doing—they prepare you to earn bread in a better way, in an easier way, in a more comfortable way, with less effort, with less hardship. It is a very primitive kind of education: it does not prepare you for life.

Hence you see so many robots walking around. They are perfect as clerks, as stationmasters, as deputy collectors. They are perfect, they are skillful, but if you look deep down in them they are just beggars and nothing else. They have not even tasted one bite of life. They have not known what life is, what love is, what light is. They have not known anything of godliness, they have not tasted anything of existence, they don't know how to sing and how to dance and how to celebrate. They don't know the grammar of life; they are utterly stupid. Yes, they earn—they earn more than others, they are very skillful and they go on rising higher and higher on the ladder of success—but deep down they remain empty, poor.

Education is to give you inner richness. It is not just to make you more informed; that is a very primitive idea of education. I call it primitive because it is rooted in fear, rooted in the idea that "If I am not well educated I will not be able to survive." I call it primitive because deep down it is violent: it teaches you competition, it makes you ambitious. It is nothing but a preparation for a cutthroat, competitive world where everybody is the enemy of everybody else.

Hence the world has become a madhouse. Love cannot happen. How can love happen in such a violent, ambitious, competitive world where everybody is at each other's throat? This is very primitive, because it is based in the fear that, "If I am not well educated, well protected, highly informed, I may not be able to survive in the struggle of life." It takes life only as a struggle.

My vision of education is that life should not be taken as a struggle for survival; life should be taken as a celebration. Life should not be only competition, life should be joy too. Singing and dancing and poetry and music and painting, and all that is available in the world . . . education should prepare you to fall in tune with it, with the trees, with the birds, with the sky, with the sun and the moon.

And education should prepare you to be yourself. Right now it prepares you to be an imitator; it teaches you how to be like others. This is *mis*education. Right education will teach you how to be yourself, authentically yourself. You are unique. There is nobody like you, has never been, will never be. This is a great respect that existence has showered on you. This is your glory, that you are unique. Don't become imitative, don't become carbon copies.

But that's what your so-called education goes on doing: it makes carbon copies; it destroys your original face. The word "education" has two meanings, and both are beautiful. One meaning is very well known, although not practiced at all; that is, to draw something out of you. "Education" means to draw out that which is within you, to make your potential actual, like you draw water from a well.

But this is not being practiced. On the contrary, things are being poured into you, not drawn out of you. Geography and history and science and mathematics, they go on pouring into you. You become parrots. You have been treated like computers; just as they feed the computers, they feed you. Your educational institutions are places where things are crammed into your head.

Real education will be to bring out what is hidden in you—what existence has put in you as a treasure—to discover it, to reveal it, to make you luminous.

Another meaning of the word, which is even far deeper: "Education" comes from the word *educare;* it means to lead you from darkness to light. A tremendously significant meaning: to lead you from darkness to light. Man lives in darkness, in unconsciousness—

and man is capable of becoming full of light. The flame is there; it has to be provoked. The consciousness is there, but it has to be awakened. You have been given all, you have brought it with you; but the whole idea that you have become a human being just by having a human body is wrong, and that idea has been the cause of tremendous mischief down the ages.

Man is born just as an opportunity, as an occasion. And very few people attain: a Jesus, a Buddha, a Mohammed, a Bahaudin. Very few people, few and far between, really become human—when they become full of light and there is no darkness left, when there is no unconsciousness lingering anywhere in your soul, when all is light, when you are just awareness. Then life is a benediction.

Education is to bring you from darkness to light. That's what I am doing here. I am teaching you to be yourself. I am teaching you to be fearless; I am teaching you not to yield to social pressure; I am teaching you not to be a conformist. I am teaching you not to hanker for comfort and convenience, because if you hanker for comfort and convenience the society will give them to you, but at a cost. And the cost is great: you get convenience but you lose your consciousness. You get comfort but you lose your soul. You can have respectability, but then you are not true to yourself; you are a pseudo human being. You have betrayed existence and yourself.

But the society wants you to betray yourself. The society wants to use you as a machine, the society wants you to be obedient. The society does not need you to function as an intelligent being, because an intelligent being will behave in an intelligent way and there may be moments when he will say, "No, I cannot do this."

For example, if you are really intelligent and aware, you cannot be part of any army—impossible. To be part of any army you need, as a basic requirement, unintelligence. That's why in the army they manage in every way to destroy your intelligence. Years are needed to destroy your intelligence; they call it "training." Stupid orders have to be followed: right turn, left turn, march forward, march backward—this and that—and they go on and on every day, morning, evening. Slowly, slowly the person becomes a robot, he starts functioning like a machine.

I have heard that a woman went to a psychoanalyst and said, "I am very much worried, I cannot sleep. My husband is a colonel in the army. Whenever he comes home for holidays it becomes a nightmare for me. Whenever he is sleeping on his right side he snores, and snores so loudly that not only am I disturbed, even the neighbors are disturbed. Can you suggest something to me? What should I do?"

The psychoanalyst thought it over, and then he said, "Do one thing. Tonight try this, maybe it will work," and he gave her a recipe and it worked. And the recipe was simple—he said to her, "When he starts snoring, just tell him, 'Left turn.'"

She could not believe it, but when she did it, it worked— even in his sleep. He snored only on his right side, and when she said in his ear, slowly, not very loudly, softly, "Left turn," just out of the old habit he turned left. The snoring stopped, even in sleep.

The whole training in the army is to destroy your consciousness, is to make you an automatic machine. Then you can go and kill. Otherwise, if you are still carrying a little bit of intelligence, you will see the other person that you are killing is innocent; he has not done anything to you or to anybody. And he must have a wife at home who is waiting for him to come back; he may have small children, and they will become beggars; he may have an old mother or an old father, they may go mad. "Why am I killing this man? Because the officer says, 'Start killing. Fire!'"

An intelligent person will not be able to fire. An intelligent person may choose to die himself rather than to kill innocent people. Because some foolish politician wants to get involved in a war, because some politician wants to have some power, because of some stupid statements of the politicians, the war has started. He will not kill!

This I call education: to make people more intelligent. And that's what I am doing here. If this fire spreads, this old, rotten society cannot survive. It survives on your unconsciousness, it lives on your unconsciousness.

• • •

The education that has existed up to now has not been true. It has not served humanity; on the contrary, it has served the vested interests. It has served the past. The teacher has been an agent of the past. He functions as a mediator to give past beliefs, orientations, assumptions, to the coming generation—to contaminate, to pollute the new consciousness that is arising on the horizon.

And because of education, man's evolution has been very haphazard, zigzag. But up to now there was no other way, because there was one thing in the past: knowledge grew so slowly that it was almost the same for centuries. So the teacher was very efficient in doing his job. Whatsoever was known was almost static; it was not growing. But now there is a knowledge explosion. Things are changing so fast that the whole education system has become outdated, outmoded. It has to be dropped, and a totally new education system has to come into existence. Only now is it possible—up to now it was not possible.

You will have to understand what I mean by the knowledge explosion. Imagine a clock face with sixty minutes on it. These sixty minutes represent three thousand years of human history; or each minute, fifty years; or each second, approximately one year. On this scale there were no significant media changes until about nine minutes ago. At that time the printing press came in. About three minutes ago, the telegraph, photograph, and the locomotive. Two minutes ago, the telephone, rotary press, motion pictures, automobile, airplane, and radio. One minute ago, the talking picture. Television has appeared in the last ten seconds, the computer in the last five, and the communication satellites in the last second. The laser beam appeared only a fraction of a second ago.

This is what some people call the knowledge explosion. Change is not new; what is new is the degree of change. And that makes all the difference, because at a certain point quantitative changes become qualitative changes.

If you heat water, up to ninety-nine-point-nine degrees it is still water—maybe hot, but still water. Just point-one degree more is needed and the water starts evaporating, and there happens a qualitative change. Just a few seconds before, the water was visible, now it is invisible. Just a few seconds before, the water was flowing downward, now it is rising upward. It has transcended the pull of gravitation, it is no longer under the law of gravitation.

Remember, at a certain point the quantitative change becomes qualitative. And that's what has happened. Change is not new, it is not news; change has always been happening. But the rate of change is immensely new; it has not happened like this before. The difference between a fatal and a therapeutic dose of strychnine is only a matter of degree—that's what Norbert Wiener says. The poison can function as a medicine in a smaller dose, but the same medicine will become fatal if you give a bigger dose. At a certain point it is no longer medicine, it is poison.

Change is so tremendous now that the teacher cannot serve anymore in the past style, education cannot serve anymore in the past way. The past way was to help people to memorize. Education up to now has not been education in intelligence but only in memory, in remembrance. The past generation transferred all its knowledge to the new generation, and the new generation was to remember it. So people who had good memories were thought to be intelligent. That is not necessarily so. There have been geniuses whose memory was almost nil. Albert Einstein didn't have a good memory. There have been people whose memory was miraculous, but they had no intelligence at all.

Memory is a mechanical thing in your mind. Intelligence is the consciousness. Intelligence is part of your spirit, memory is part of your brain. Memory belongs to the body, intelligence belongs to you.

Intelligence has to be taught now, because change is happening so fast that memory won't do. By the time you have memorized something it is already out of date. And that is what is happening: the education is failing, universities are failing, because they still go on persisting in the old way. They have learned a trick; for three thousand years they have been doing this, and now they have learned it so deeply that they don't know what else they can do.

Now, just giving old information to the children, which will not make them capable of living in the future but will hamper their growth, is dangerous. Now they need intelligence to live with the fast change that is happening. Just one hundred years ago, there were millions of people who had never gone outside of their town, or never went more than fifty miles away from their town. Millions lived in the same place forever, from birth to death. Now everything is changing. In America the average person lives only three years in one place, and that is the time limit for marriage too—three years. Then one starts changing one's town, one's job, one's wife, one's husband. This is a totally new world that you are living in. And your education simply makes you walking encyclopedias, but outdated.

The difference is not new—what is new is the degree of change.

On our clock face, about three minutes ago there developed a qualitative difference in the character of change: change changed. We have to teach intelligence now, so that we can make the children capable of living with the new things that will be happening every day. Don't burden them with that which is not going to be of any use in the future. The old generation has not to teach what it has learned; the old generation has to help the child to be more intelligent so that he can be capable of spontaneously responding to the new realities that will be coming. The old generation cannot even dream about what those realities will be.

Your children may be living on the moon; they will have a totally different atmosphere to live in. Your children may be living in the sky, because the earth is becoming too populated. Your children may have to live underground or under the sea. Nobody knows how your children will have to live. They may live only on tablets, vitamin pills . . . they will be living in a totally different world. So it is of no use just to go on giving them encyclopedic knowledge from the past. We have to prepare them to face new realities.

We have to prepare them in awareness, in meditativeness. Then education will be true. Then it will not serve the past and the dead; it will serve the future. It will serve the living.

In my vision, to be true the education has to be subversive, rebellious. Up to now it has been orthodox, up to now it has been part of the establishment. True education has to teach things which no other institution does. It has to become the anti-entropy business.

The state, the establishment, and all the institutions of the society, all prevent growth—remember it. Why do they prevent growth? Because every growth brings challenge, and they are settled. And who wants to be unsettled? Those who are in power would not like anything new to happen, because that will change the power balance. Those who are in power would not like any new thing to be released, because the new thing will make new people powerful. Each new knowledge brings new power into the world, and the older generation would not like to lose its grip, its domination.

Education has to serve revolution. But ordinarily it serves the government and the priest and the church. In a very subtle way, it prepares slaves—slaves for the state, slaves for the church. The real purpose of education should be to subvert outmoded attitudes, beliefs and assumptions that no longer serve growth and humanity, and are positively harmful and suicidal.

> An interviewer once asked Ernest Hemingway, "Isn't there any one essential ingredient you can identify which makes a great writer?"
>
> Hemingway replied, "Yes, there is. In order to be a great writer a person must have a built-in, shockproof, crap detector."

That's what my idea of true education is. The children should be trained, disciplined, so that they can detect crap. A really intelligent person is a crap detector. He immediately knows, the moment someone says something, whether it is significant or just holy cow dung.

The evolution of human consciousness is nothing but a long history of struggle against the veneration of crap. People go on worshipping, venerating crap. Ninety-nine percent of their beliefs are just lies. Ninety-nine percent of their beliefs are anti-human, anti-life. Ninety-nine percent of their beliefs are so primitive, so barbarous, so utterly ignorant that it is unbelievable how people go on believing in them.

The true education will help you to drop all nonsense—howsoever ancient, respectable, revered. It will teach you the real. It will not teach you any superstition but how to live more joyously.

It will teach you life-affirmation. It will teach you reverence for life and for nothing else. It will teach you how to be deeply in love with existence. It will not be only of the mind, it will be also of the heart.

It will also help you to become a no-mind. That is the dimension that is missing from education. It simply teaches you to become more and more entangled in mental concepts, lost in mind. Mind is good, useful, but it is not your wholeness. There is heart too, which is in fact far more important than the mind—because the mind can create better technology, can give you better machines, better roads, better houses, but cannot make you a better human being. It cannot make you more loving, more poetic, more graceful. It cannot give you the joy of life, the celebration. It cannot help you to become a song and a dance.

The true education has to teach you the ways of the heart, too. And the true education has also to teach you the transcendental. Mind is for science, heart for art, poetry, music, and the transcendental for religion. Unless an education serves all these things, it is not true. And no educational system has yet done it.

It is not surprising that many young people are dropping out of your colleges, your universities—because they can see it is all crap, they can see it is all stupid.

No other institution can do it, only education can do it: universities should sow the seeds of mutation—because a new man has to arrive on the earth.

The first rays have already reached. The new human being is arriving every day and we have to prepare the earth to receive it, and with the new human being a new humanity and a new world. There is no other possibility except education to receive the new man, to prepare the ground. And if we cannot prepare the ground, we are doomed.

The experiments we are doing here are really an effort to create the new kind of university. This has to be done, and this has to be done all over the earth in many places. This experiment has to be done in every country. Only a few will take the challenge, but those few will be the heralds. Those few will declare the new age, the new man, the new humanity.

. . .

Walt Whitman has written:

When I heard the learn'd astronomer;
When the proofs, the figures, were ranged in columns before me;
When I was shown the charts and the diagrams,
to add, divide and measure them;
When I, sitting, heard the astronomer, where he lectured
with much applause in the lecture-room,
How soon, unaccountable, I became tired and sick;
Till rising and gliding out, I wander'd off by myself,
In the mystical moist night air, and from time to time
Look'd up in perfect silence at the stars.

The new education, the true education, has not only to teach you mathematics, history, geography, science; it also has to teach you the real morality: aesthetics. I call aesthetics the real morality—sensitivity to feel the beautiful, because godliness comes as beauty. In a rose flower or in a lotus, in the sunrise or in the sunset, in the stars, the birds singing in the early morning, or the dewdrops, a bird on the wing. . . . True education has to bring you closer and closer to nature because only by coming closer and closer to nature will you be coming closer and closer to the divine.

If intellect is such an obstacle in the journey toward self-realization, is not then training and sharpening of it just useless? Is it not possible that because of their innocence and expressiveness children should be helped to move into meditation directly, without imparting them any training in the intellect?

It is worth consideration, it is significant, and the question naturally arises that if intellect is such a big obstacle, why train it in the first place? Why not introduce children to meditation while they are still innocent and simple, instead of sending them to university? Instead of shaping their logic and thinking faculty, instead of educating them, why not drown them into meditation in their innocence and simplicity? If intellect is an obstacle, why help it grow? Why not get rid of it before developing it?

It would have been all right if intellect was only an obstacle. But an obstacle can also become a stepping-stone. You are walking on a pathway and there is a huge rock lying on the pathway. Now, this is an obstacle, and you may return from there thinking the pathway does not go anywhere farther. But if you climb on the rock, a new pathway is revealed—which is totally on a different level from the previous lower one. A new dimension opens up.

The unintelligent one will return from that place taking the rock as an obstacle. The intelligent one will use the rock as a ladder. And intelligence, wisdom, is a totally different thing from what we call intellect.

Without training the intellect the children will remain like animals. It is not that they will become wise, they will remain like wild animals. Of course, they wouldn't have the obstacle, but they wouldn't have any means to climb up either. In itself, neither is the stone an obstacle, nor is the ladder a help.

So it is necessary that every child goes through the intellectual training. And the more beautiful this training, the sharper this training—the stronger, the bigger, the vaster this rock of intellect—

the better, because in the same proportion it is a means to rise to greater heights. The one who gets crushed under this rock is the scholar. The one who stands on top of this rock is the sage. And the one who, out of fear, does not even come close to the rock, is the ignorant.

The ignorant one's intellect was never trained; the scholar's intellect was trained but he could not go beyond it; the wise one's intellect was not only trained, he also managed to go beyond it.

Avoidance would not help; one has to go through and beyond. And whatsoever experience one goes through, it intensifies one, it makes one luminous.

So the intellect of the child will have to be trained; his logic will have to be sharpened so that it becomes like a sword. Then, whether he will cut himself with the sword, commit suicide, or save somebody's life, all depends on his intelligence.

Logic is just a means. We can use it for destroying life—then it is destructive; we can use it for creating life—then it is creative. But one thing is certain: just keeping children deprived of intellect will not make them intelligent. They would be innocent like animals but they would not be meditative like sages.

It has happened sometimes that a child has been taken away to the forest by some wolf. About forty years ago, two such girls were found in the forests near Calcutta. Some ten years ago, another child who had been brought up by wolves was found in a forest near Lucknow. This child was quite grown up; he was nearly fourteen years of age. This child had never received any human education, he had never known any school, he had not known any human company; he was taken away by the wolves while he was still an infant in his cradle, so he grew up with the wolves. He was unable to even stand up on his two feet, because that too is a part of human training. Don't ever think that you are standing on your two feet just on your own; it has been taught to you.

The human body is structured to walk on all fours. No child walks on two feet after his birth, he walks on four; to walk on the two feet is a learning. If you ask scientists, physiologists, they say a very strange thing. They say that the human body can never be healthy like that of animals, because the human body was meant to walk on four legs, and he has messed up everything; he is walking on two legs, so the whole system is disturbed. It is like a car that was not designed for going up a mountain; gravitational laws are disturbed—because when you walk on the ground on all fours you are balanced, your weight is equally distributed on four, and your body is parallel to the gravitation, there is equal amount of gravitational force all along your spine and there is no trouble. But when you stand up on your two legs, everything is disturbed. The blood has to flow upward, the lungs have to work extra, unnecessarily. All the time there is a struggle with the force of gravity. The earth is pulling downward. So if person dies of heart failure, there is no wonder in it. Animals rarely die of heart failure; heart weakness does not develop in healthy animals and it cannot be avoided in human beings. It is a miracle if it does not happen to some people; otherwise, in general, it is bound to happen because all this reverse work of pumping the blood is being done continuously—which is a must, but nature had not designed things this way.

So that boy who lived with the wolves could not walk on two feet, he only used to run on all fours. And his running was also not like that of human beings, it was like that of wolves. He used to eat raw meat like wolves. He was very powerful—even eight strong men would find it difficult to hold and tie him down—and he was almost a wolf. He may bite, snatch off a portion of your flesh—he was ferocious! He had not become a meditative saint, all that he had become was a wild animal. Similar incidents have happened in the West also: children being brought up in the forests by animals, so they were found as animals.

Then efforts were made to train this boy. For six months, all kinds of massages and electric treatments were given, and he could barely be made to stand upon his two feet, and just a little lapse and he would be back to his four—because it is very troublesome to stand on two. You have no idea of the fun of standing on all fours, so you are standing on your two and suffering.

The boy was given a name. They got tired of teaching him and all he could learn and utter before dying was a single word: Rama. He would just tell his name. Within one and a half years he died. The scientists who were studying the boy say he died because of all this training, because he was nothing more than a child of some wild animal.

This also shows how much of a child's life we may simply be killing by sending them to school. We kill their joyousness, we kill their wildness. That is the whole trouble in the schools. A class of thirty children—those thirty wild animals—we hand over to one teacher. In the teacher's hands has fallen the task of making them civilized. This is why there is no other profession like the profession of teaching. There is no other human being more distressed than a teacher. Their job is really a difficult one!

But these children will have to be educated; otherwise they will not be able to become human beings. Innocent they will be, but that innocence will be that of ignorance. A man is also innocent because of not knowing, but when he becomes innocent after knowing, then blooms the flower of life.

Training of the intellect is necessary; then transcendence of intellect is necessary.

And how will you lose what you don't even have? How can you experience the peace Einstein will experience by dropping his intellect? That peace will be incomparable, because that will be the peace after the storm. Your storm has not come yet. The taste one feels in throwing the intellect aside after much intellectual gymnastics is like the taste of the pure health one feels after recovering from some sickness. Renunciation is a great bliss in the sense that the indulgence preceding it was a great misery.

Pass through the misery of intellect so that you can attain to the bliss of wisdom. Pass through the anguish of the world so that the ultimate ecstasy, awakening into the divine, can be yours.

You will have to pass through the opposites; that is the way.

THE FIVE-DIMENSIONAL EDUCATION

Education up to now has been goal-oriented: what you are learning is not important, what is important is the examination that will come a year or two years later. It makes the future more important than the present. It sacrifices the present for the future. And that becomes your very style of life; you are always sacrificing the moment for something which is not present. It creates a tremendous emptiness in life.

The commune of my vision will have a five-dimensional education.

Before I enter into those five dimensions, a few things have to be noted. One: there should not be any kind of examination as part of education but every day, every hour observation by the teachers; their remarks throughout the year will decide whether you move further or you remain a little longer in the same class. Nobody fails, nobody passes—it is just that a few people are speedy and a few people are a little bit lazy. The idea of failure creates a deep wound of inferiority, and the idea of being successful also creates a different kind of disease, that of superiority.

Nobody is inferior, and nobody is superior. One is just oneself, incomparable. So examinations will not have any place. That will change the whole perspective from the future to the present. What you are doing right this moment will be decisive, not five questions at the end of two years. Of thousands of things you will pass through during these two years, each will be decisive; so the education will not be goal-oriented.

The teacher has been of immense importance in the past, because the teacher had passed all the examinations, had accumulated knowledge. But the situation has changed—and this is one of the problems, that situations change but our responses remain the old ones. Now the knowledge explosion is so vast, so tremendous, so speedy, that you cannot write a big book on any scientific subject because by the time your book is complete, it will be out of date. New facts, new discoveries will have made it irrelevant. So now science has to depend on articles, on periodicals, not on books. The teacher was educated thirty years earlier. In thirty years everything has changed, and he goes on repeating what he was taught. He is out of date and he is making his students out of date. So in my vision, the teacher has no place. Instead of teachers there will be guides, and the difference has to be understood: the guide will tell you where, in the library, to find the latest information on the subject.

Teaching should not be done in the old-fashioned way, because television can do it in a far better way, can bring the latest information without any problems. The teacher has to appeal to your ears; television appeals directly to your eyes and the impact is far greater, because the eyes absorb 80 percent of your life situations—they are the most alive part of you. If you can see something there is no need to memorize it; but if you listen to something you have to memorize it. Almost 98 percent of education can be delivered through television, and the questions that students will ask can be answered by computers. The teacher should be only a guide to show you the right channel, to show you how to use the computer, how to find the latest book. The function of teachers will be totally different. They will not be imparting knowledge to you, they will be making you aware of the contemporary knowledge, of the latest knowledge. The teacher will be only a guide.

With these considerations, I divide education into five dimensions. The first is informative, like history, geography, and many other subjects which can be dealt with by television and computer together. The second part should be sciences. They can be imparted by television and computer too, but they are more complicated and the human guide will be more necessary.

In the first dimension also come languages. Every person in the world should know at least two languages: one is the mother tongue and the other is English as an international vehicle for communication. Languages can also be taught more accurately by television—the accent, the grammar, everything can be taught more correctly than by human teachers in the classroom. We can create in the world an atmosphere of brotherhood: language connects people and language disconnects, too. There is right now no international language.

English is the most widespread language, and people should drop their prejudices—they should look at the reality. There have been many efforts to create languages to avoid the prejudices—the Spanish people can say their language should be the international language because it is spoken by more people than almost any other language . . . To avoid these prejudices, languages like Esperanto have been created. But no created language has been able to function. There are a few things which grow, which cannot be created; a language is a growth of thousands of years. Esperanto and other created languages are so artificial that all those efforts have failed.

But it is absolutely necessary to speak two languages—first, the mother tongue, because there are feelings and nuances which you can say only in the mother tongue. . . .

One of my professors, a world traveler who has been a professor of philosophy in many countries, used to say that in a foreign language you can do everything, but when it comes to a fight or to expressing love, you feel that you are not being true and sincere to your feelings. So for your feelings and for your sincerity, your mother tongue . . . which you imbibe with the milk of the mother, which becomes part of your blood and bones and marrow. But that is not enough—that creates small groups of people and makes others strangers.

One international language is absolutely necessary as a basis for one world, for one humanity. So two languages should be absolutely necessary for everybody. That will come in the first dimension.

The second is the inquiry into scientific subjects, which is tremendously important because it is half of reality, the outside reality. And the third will be what is missing in present-day education, the art of living. People have taken it for granted that they know what love is. They don't know . . . and by the time they know, it is too late. Every child should be helped to transform his anger, hatred, jealousy, into love.

An important part of the third dimension should also be a sense of humor. Our so-called education makes people sad and serious. And if one-third of your life is wasted in a university in being sad and serious, it becomes ingrained; you forget the language of laughter—and the person who forgets the language of laughter has forgotten much of life.

So love, laughter, and an acquaintance with life and its wonders, its mysteries . . . these birds singing in the trees should not go unheard. The trees and the flowers and the stars should have a connection with your heart. The sunrise and the sunset will not be just things outside, they should be something inner, too. A reverence for life should be the foundation of the third dimension.

People are so irreverent of life. They still go on killing animals to eat—they call it "game"; and if the animal eats them, then they call it a calamity! Strange . . . in a game, both parties should be given equal opportunity. The animals are without weapons and you have machine guns or arrows. A great reverence for life should be taught, because life is God and there is no other God than life itself. And joy, laughter, a sense of humor—in short, a dancing spirit.

The fourth dimension should be of art and creativity: painting, music, craftsmanship, pottery, masonry, anything that is creative. All areas of creativity should be allowed; the students can choose. There should be only a few things compulsory—for example, an international language should be compulsory; a certain capacity to earn your livelihood should be compulsory; a certain creative art should be compulsory. You can choose from the whole rainbow of creative arts, because unless you learn how to create, you never become a part of existence, which is constantly creative. By being creative one becomes divine; creativity is the only prayer.

And the fifth dimension should be the art of dying. In this fifth dimension will be all the meditations, so that you can know there is no death, so that you can become aware of an eternal life inside you. This should be absolutely essential, because everybody has to die; nobody can avoid it. And under the big umbrella of meditation, you can be introduced to Zen, to Tao, to Yoga, to Hassidism, to all kinds and all possibilities that have existed, but which education has not taken any care of. In this fifth dimension you should also be made aware of the martial arts like aikido, jujitsu, judo— the art of self-defense without weapons—and these are not only self-defense but simultaneously a meditation too.

The new commune will have a full education, a whole education. All that is essential should be compulsory, and all that is nonessential should be optional. One can choose from the options, which will be many. And once the basics are fulfilled, then you have to learn something you enjoy—music, dance, painting. You have to know something to go inward, to know yourself. And all this can be done very easily without any difficulty.

I have been a professor myself, and I resigned from the university with a note saying, "This is not education, this is sheer stupidity; you are not teaching anything significant." But this insignificant education prevails all over the world—it makes no difference, in the Soviet Union or in America. Nobody has looked for a more whole, a total education. In this sense almost everybody is uneducated; even those who have great degrees are uneducated in the vaster areas of life. A few are more uneducated, a few are less, but everybody is uneducated. But to find an educated man is impossible, because education as a whole does not exist anywhere.

. . .

Ordinarily that which is called education is almost against meditation. It should not be so but it is so. The original meaning of the word *education* is not against meditation. To educate means whatsoever is hidden in the individual has to be drawn out. The individual has to flower—that is the original meaning of education.

That is what meditation is, too: you have to flower in your own being. You don't know what you are going to be, you don't know what flowers will come to you, what will be their color and what will be their perfume—you don't know. You move into the unknown. You simply trust life energy. It has given birth to you, it is your foundation, it is your being; you trust it. You know that you are a child of this universe and this universe, if it has given birth to you, will take care, too.

When you trust yourself you trust the whole universe also. And this universe is beautiful. Just see . . . so many flowers are born in this universe; how can you mistrust it? Such tremendous beauty is all around; how can you mistrust it? Such grandeur, such grace, from a small dust particle to the stars. Such symmetry, such harmony, how can you mistrust it?

Basho has said, "If flowers are born out of this universe, then I trust it." Right? That is enough logic, a great argument: "If this universe can give birth to so many beautiful flowers, if a rose is possible, I trust it. If a lotus is possible, I trust it."

Education is a trust in yourself and in existence, allowing unfoldment of whatsoever is hidden in you, bringing whatsoever is in, out. But nobody is bothered about you. The society is bothered about its own ideas, ideologies, prejudices, technology; they go on forcing you. Your head is used as a hollow place, and they provide the furniture. Ordinarily education, or whatsoever is available in the name of education, is nothing but stuffing your mind with knowledge—because knowledge has some utility. Nobody is bothered about you, nobody is bothered about your destiny. They need more doctors, they need more engineers, they need more generals, they need more technicians, plumbers, electricians. They need them, so they force you to become a plumber or they force you to become a doctor, or they force you to become an engineer. I am not saying there is something wrong with being an engineer or a doctor, but there is certainly something wrong if it is forced from the outside. If somebody flowers into a doctor, then you will see a great healing happening around him. Then he will be a born healer. He will really be a physician, his touch will be golden. He is born to be that.

But when it is forced from the outside and one takes it as a profession, because one has to live and one has to learn and earn one's living, one takes it over. Then one is crippled and crushed under the weight. One simply goes on dragging and dragging, and one day dies. There has never been a moment of celebration in that life. Of course, the person will leave much money for his children to become doctors in their own turn, to go to university, to the same university where he was destroyed. And his children will do the same to their children, and this is how things go on being transferred from one generation to another. No, I don't call this education. It is crime. It is really a miracle that in spite of this education sometimes a Buddha flowers in the world. It is a miracle. It is simply unbelievable how somebody can escape out of it: it is a methodology to kill you, it is arranged in such a way. And small children are caught in the mechanism of it, not knowing where they are going, not knowing what is being made of them. By the time they become aware, they are completely corrupted and destroyed. By the time they can think about what to do with their lives, they are almost incapable of moving in any other direction.

By the time you are twenty-five or thirty, half the life is gone. Now to change seems to be too risky. You have become a doctor, your practice is going well; suddenly one day you realize that this is not the thing you were meant to be. This is not for you—but now what to do? So go on pretending that you are a doctor. And if the doctor is not happy in being a doctor, he is not going to help any patient. He may drug the patient, he may give medicine, but he is not going to really be a healing force. When a doctor is really a doctor, he is a born doctor . . . and everybody is a born something. You may miss it, you may not even know it. Somebody is a born poet; and you cannot make a poet. There is no way to manufacture poets. Somebody is a born painter; you cannot manufacture painters. But things are very wrongly placed: the painter is working as a doctor, the doctor is working as a painter. The politician is there: maybe he could have been a good plumber but he has become a prime minister or a president. And the person who could have been a prime minister is a plumber.

This is why in the world there is so much chaos: everybody is wrongly placed, nobody is exactly where he should be. Right education will exactly be a path to meditation. Wrong education is a barrier to meditation because wrong education teaches you things which don't fit with you. And unless something fits with you and you fit with it, you can never be healthy and whole. You will suffer.

Ordinarily, when an educated person becomes interested in meditation he has to unlearn whatsoever he has learned. He has to go back to his childhood again and start from there, from the ABCs. That's why my insistence is for certain meditations in which you can again become a child. When you dance you are more like a child than like a grown-up person.

People who have some respectability become very stuck because they cannot do anything—they cannot risk their respectability. They are afraid. They are not happy, they don't know what bliss is, they don't exactly know what being alive means—but they are respectable. So they cling to their respectability and then die. They never live; they die before they ever start living. There are many people who die before they have ever lived.

My meditations are to bring you back to your childhood—when you were not respectable, when you could do crazy things, when you were innocent, uncorrupted by the society, when you had not learned any tricks of the world, when you were otherworldly, unworldly. I would like you to go back to that point; from there, start again. And this is your life. Respectability or money are booby prizes, they are not real prizes. Don't be deceived by them.

You cannot eat respectability, and you cannot eat money, and you cannot eat prestige. They are just games: meaningless, stupid, mediocre. If you are intelligent enough you will understand that you have to live your life and you are not to bother about other things. All other considerations are meaningless: it is your life. You have to live it authentically, lovingly, with great passion and with great compassion, with great energy. You have to become a tidal wave of bliss. Whatsoever is needed to do for it, do.

Unlearning will be needed. Unlearning means that you stop

those wrong routes, you stop moving in those wrong ways that the society has forced you, persuaded you, seduced you to go in. You take charge of your own life; you become your own master. That is the meaning of sannyas. A real sannyasin is one who does not care about others' opinion, who has decided to live his life as he wants to live it. I don't mean for you to be irresponsible. When you start living your life responsibly, you not only care about yourself, you care about others also—but in a totally different way. Now you will take every care that you don't interfere in anybody else's life—this is what responsibility is. You don't allow anybody to interfere in your life and, naturally, you will not interfere in anybody's life. You don't want anybody to guide your life, you don't want your life to be a guided tour. A guided tour is not a tour at all—you want to explore on your own. You want to move in the forest without any map, so that you can also be a discoverer, so that you can also come to some fresh spots for the first time. If you carry a map you always come to the spot where many have come before. It is never new, it is never original, it is never virgin. It is already contaminated, corrupted. Many have moved on it, a map even exists.

When I was a child, in the temple that my parents used to visit I was surprised: there were maps of heaven and hell and *moksha,* the ultimate liberation. One day I told my father, "If maps exist about *moksha*, then I am not interested in it."

He said, "Why?" I said, "If maps exist, then it is already rotten. Many people have reached there, even mapmakers have reached there. Everything is measured and they know every spot, named and labeled. This seems to be just an extension of the same old world. It is nothing new. I would like to move in a world that has no map. I would like to be an explorer." That day I stopped going into the temple.

My father asked me, "Why don't you come now?"

I said, "You remove those maps. I cannot tolerate those maps there. They are very offensive. Just think about it: Even *moksha* is measured? Then is there nothing immeasurable!"

All the buddhas have said that truth is immeasurable; all the buddhas have said that truth is not only unknown, it is unknowable. It is an uncharted sea: you take your small boat and you go into the uncharted sea. You take the adventure. It is risky, it is dangerous. But in risk and danger the soul flowers, becomes integrated.

To me, if education is right it will be just a part of meditation; meditation will be the last point in it. If education is right, then universities should not be against the universe. They should be just training places, jumping boards into the universe. If education is right it will be concerned about your bliss, your happiness, music, love, poetry, dance. It will teach you how to unfold. It will help you to come out of your own being, to flower, to grow, to spread, to expand.

Education is religious if it makes you courageous enough to accept yourself, and live your life, and become an offering to existence in your own way, in your own unique way.

. . .

Listening to the birds, I remember . . . just outside my classroom in the high school there were beautiful mango trees. And mango trees are where cuckoos make their nests. This is a cuckoo that is calling now, and there is nothing sweeter than the sound of a cuckoo.

So I used to sit by the window, looking out at the birds, at the trees, and my teachers were very annoyed. They said, "You have to look at the blackboard."

I said, "It is my life, and I have every right to choose where to look. Outside is so beautiful—the birds singing, and the flowers, and the trees, and the sun coming through the trees—that I don't think your blackboard can be a competitor."

One teacher was so angry that he told me, "Then you can go out and stand there outside the window unless you are ready to look at the blackboard—because I am teaching you mathematics, and you are looking at the trees and the birds."

I said, "This is a great reward you are giving me, not a punishment." And I said good-bye to him.

He said, "What do you mean?"

I said, "I will never come in, I will be standing every day outside the window."

He said, "You must be crazy. I will report to your father, to your family: 'You are wasting money on him, and he's standing outside.'"

I said, "You can do anything you want to do. I know how to manage things with my father. And he knows perfectly well that if I have decided then I will remain outside the window—nothing can change it."

The principal used to see me standing outside the window every day when he came for a round. He was puzzled at what I was doing there every day. On the third or fourth day he came to me, and he said, "What are you doing? Why do you go on standing here?"

I said, "I have been rewarded."

He said, "Rewarded? For what?"

I said, "You just stand by my side and listen to the songs of the birds. And the beauty of the trees. . . . Do you think looking at the blackboard and that stupid teacher . . . because only stupid people become teachers; they cannot find any other employment. Mostly they are third-class graduates. So neither do I want to look at that teacher, nor do I want to look at the blackboard. As far as mathematics is concerned, you need not be worried—I will manage it. But I cannot miss this beauty."

He stood by my side, and he said, "Certainly it is beautiful. I have been a principal for twenty years in this school, and I never came here. I agree with you that this is a reward. As far as mathematics is concerned, I am an MSc in mathematics. You can come to my house anytime and I will teach you mathematics—continue to stand outside."

So I got a better teacher, the principal of the school, who was a better mathematician. And my mathematics teacher was very much puzzled. He thought that I would get tired after a few days, but the whole month passed. Then he came out, and he said, "I am sorry, because it hurts me continuously the whole time I am in the class that I have forced you to stand out here. And you have not done any harm. You can sit inside and look wherever you want."

I said, "Now it is too late."

He said, "What do you mean?"

I said, "I mean that now I enjoy being outside. Sitting behind the window only a very small portion of the trees and the birds is available; here all the thousands of mango trees are available. And as far as mathematics is concerned, the principal is teaching me himself; every evening I go to him."

He said, "What?"

I said, "Yes, because he agreed with me that this is a reward."

He went directly to the principal and said, "This is not good. I had punished him and you are encouraging him." The principal said, "Forget punishment and encouragement—you should also stand outside sometime. Now I cannot wait; otherwise I used to go for the round as a routine, but now I cannot wait. The first thing I have to do is to go for the round and stay with that boy and look at the trees.

"For the first time, I have learned that there are better things than mathematics—the sounds of the birds, the flowers, the green trees, the sun rays coming through the trees, the wind blowing, singing its song through the trees. Once in a while you should also go and accompany him."

He came back very sorry and said, "The principal told me what has happened, so what should I do?" He asked me, "Should I take the whole class out?"

I said, "That would be great. We can sit under these trees, and you can teach your mathematics. But I am not going to come in the class, even if you make me fail—which you cannot do, because I now know more mathematics than any student in the class. And I have a better teacher. You are a third-class BSc, and he is a first-class gold medalist MSc."

For a few days he thought about it, and one morning when I went there I saw that the whole class was sitting under the trees. I said, "Your heart is still alive; mathematics has not killed it."

Would you speak on religious education?

Every child is brought up, conditioned, into a certain religion. It is one of the biggest crimes against humanity. Nothing can be a bigger crime than to pollute the mind of an innocent child with ideas that are going to become hindrances in his discovery of life.

The moment you want to discover something, you have to be absolutely unprejudiced. You cannot discover religion as a Mohammedan, as a Christian, as a Hindu—no. These are the ways to prevent you from discovering religion.

Every society, until now, has been trying to indoctrinate every child. Before the child becomes capable of asking questions, he is being given answers. Do you see the stupidity of it? The child has not asked the question, and you are providing him with an answer. What you are doing in reality is killing the very possibility of the question arising. You have filled his mind with the answer. And unless he has his own question, how can he have his own answer? The quest has to be sincerely his. It cannot be borrowed, it cannot be inherited.

But this nonsense has continued for centuries. The priest is interested, the politician is interested, the parents are interested in making something of you before you can discover who you are. They are afraid that if you discover who you are, you will be a rebel, you will be dangerous to the vested interests. Then you will be an individual, living in his own right, not living a borrowed life.

They are so afraid, that before the child becomes capable of asking, inquiring, they start stuffing his mind with all kinds of nonsense. The child is helpless. He naturally believes in the mother, in the father, and of course he believes in the priest in whom the father and mother believe. The great phenomenon of doubt has not arisen yet.

And it is one of the most precious things in life, to doubt, because unless you doubt you cannot discover.

You have to sharpen your doubting forces so that you can cut through all rubbish and you can ask questions that nobody can answer. Only your own quest, inquiry, will help you to come to the realization of them. The religious question is not something which can be answered by somebody else. Nobody else can love on your behalf. Nobody else can live on your behalf.

You have to live your life, and you have to seek and search the fundamental questions of life.

Unless you discover yourself, there is no joy, no ecstasy. If God is just given to you, ready-made, it is not worth anything, it is valueless. But that's how it is being done.

What you call religious ideas are not religious, but only superstitions carried down the ages—so long, that just their ancientness has made them appear like truth.

It is impossible for a child to doubt—all these people are wrong? And these are not the only people. Their parents, and their parents, for thousands of years, have been believing in these truths. They all cannot be wrong. "And I, a small child against this whole humanity . . ." He cannot gather courage. He starts repressing any possibility of doubt. And everybody else helps to repress doubt because, "Doubt is from the devil. Doubt is a great, perhaps the greatest, sin. Belief is virtue. Believe and you will find; doubt, and you have missed on the very first step."

The truth is just the opposite. Believe and you will never find, and whatsoever you find will be nothing but the projection of your own belief—it will not be truth.

What has truth to do with your believing?

Doubt, and doubt totally, because doubt is a cleansing process. It takes out all junk from your mind. It makes you again innocent, again the child that has been destroyed by the parents, by the priests, by the politicians, by the pedagogues. You have to discover that child again. You have to start from that point.

I was born in a Jaina family. In Jainism, God is not believed in; there is no God as creator. Because the conditioning of Jainism does not enforce the idea of God on its children, no Jaina child, or an old Jaina ever asks, "Who created the world?" They have been conditioned, from the very beginning, that the world exists from eternity to eternity; there is nobody who is a creator, and there is no need. Hence the question does not arise.

The Buddhist never asks the question, "What is God, where is God?" because Buddhism does not believe in God—so the child has been conditioned in that way. When you ask about God, you think that it is your question—it is not! You may have been born in a Hindu family, in a Christian family, in a Jewish family, and they have conditioned your mind that there is a God. They have given a certain image of God, certain ideas about God. And they have created you with such fear that to doubt is dangerous. A small, tiny kid is being made afraid of the eternal hell where you will be thrown into fire, alive, and you will burn but you will not die. Naturally the doubt does not seem to be so significant to take such risk. And you are motivated that if you believe, simply believe, all pleasures, all joys of life are yours. Believe and you are on the side of God; doubt and you are on the side of the devil.

The small child is bound to buy whatsoever crap you are giving him. He is afraid. He is afraid to be alone in the night, in the house, and you are talking about eternal hell: "You go on falling and falling into darkness and deeper darkness, and there is no end to it, and you can never come out of it." Naturally the child simply shrinks from doubting, becomes so afraid that it is not worth it. And belief is so simple. Nothing is expected of you—just to believe in God, the son, the Holy Ghost . . . just to believe that Jesus is the son of God, and the messiah . . . and he has come to redeem the whole of humanity . . . and he will redeem you too. Why not be redeemed so cheaply? You are not asked much. Just believe, and everything will be settled in your favor. So why should you choose doubt? You should naturally choose belief.

This happens at such a young age, and then you go on growing. Then the belief and the conditioning and the ideas and the philosophy all go on top of it—so it is very difficult to dig and find out that there was a day when you were also full of doubt. The doubt has been crushed, put out of sight. There was a day when you were reluctant to believe, but you have been persuaded. All kinds of rewards have been placed before you.

You can persuade a little child just by giving him a toy—and you have given him the whole paradise.

If you have succeeded in persuading him to believe, you have not done a great miracle. It is very simple exploitation.

Perhaps you are doing it unknowingly; you have also been passed through the same process.

Once you close the doors of doubt you have closed the doors of reason, thinking, asking, inquiring. You are no longer really a human being. With the doors of doubt closed you are just a zombie, hypnotized, conditioned, persuaded out of fear, out of greed, to believe in things which no normal child is going to believe if all these things were not arranged.

And once you stop doubting and thinking, then you can believe anything whatsoever. Then there is no question.

Only from your innocent childhood a real inquiry into truth begins. Only from there, religion is possible.

A small boy gave the following summary of his Sunday school lesson:

"There were these Jews who had broken out of a prison camp in Egypt. They ran and ran until they came to a wide lake. The prison guards were closing in so the Jews jumped into the water and swam out to some boats that were waiting for them. The guards got in submarines and tried to torpedo the boats, but the Jews set off depth charges and blew up all the submarines and made it safely to the other side. Everybody called the admiral by his first name, Moses."

The boy's father asked, "Son are you certain that is what your teacher told you?"

"Dad," responded the boy, "if you can't believe my story, you would never believe the one the teacher told."

Now, telling children stupid stories you are not helping them to become religious; on the contrary, you are helping them to become anti-religious. When they grow up they will know that all those religious doctrines were fairy tales. Your God, your Jesus Christ, all will turn into Santa Claus later on in the child's mind— deceptions, fables, to keep children occupied. And once the children know that what you have been telling them as absolute truth is just lies and nothing else, you have destroyed something very valuable in their being. They will never become interested in religion at all.

My own observation is that the world is becoming more and more irreligious because of religious teaching.

How much do you remember that was taught to you? Nobody even remembers; everything is thrown in the garbage. You can go on teaching . . . nobody is listening. Children are helpless; they have to go to the Sunday school, so they go. They have to listen, so they listen—but they are not there. And later on they say and they know that all that was just nonsense. Now say to a child that God created the world just four thousand and four years before Jesus Christ, and the child will smile at you. The child knows that "Either you are befooling me, or you are in utter ignorance."

The world has existed for millions of years. In fact, there has never been a beginning. God is not the creator in reality, but creativity. To say to a child that God finished the world in six days and then rested on the seventh day because he was tired—now, that means that since then he has not bothered about us at all!

A man went to his tailor and asked him, "How long is it going to take for my suit to be ready? You have been promising it already for six weeks, and you say again and again, 'Come again, come again . . .' And do you know?— God created the world in only six days? In six weeks you have not been able to even create my suit."

And do you know what the tailor said? The tailor said, "Yes, I know—and look at the world, then look at my suit, and you will see the difference. The world is in a mess. This is what happens when you create something in six days."

When the Eisenbergs moved to Rome, little Hymie came home from his school in tears. He explained to his mother that the nuns were always asking these Catholic questions and how was he, a nice Jewish boy, supposed to know the answers? Mrs. Eisenberg's heart swelled with maternal sympathy. "Hymie," she said, "I'm going to embroider the answers on the inside of your shirt, and you just look down and read them the next time those nuns pick on you."

"Thanks Mum," said Hymie, and he didn't bat an eye when Sister Michele asked him who was the world's most famous virgin. "Mary," he answered.

"Very good," said the nun. "And who was her husband?"

"Joseph," answered the boy.

"I see you have been studying. Now, can you tell me the name of their son?"

"Sure," said Hymie, "Calvin Klein."

Little Ernie was getting very tired of the long sermon at the church. In a loud whisper he asked his mother, "If we give him the money now, will he let us go out?"

How can we teach children to be moral and religious?

Intelligence is the source of all religiousness and morality, and children are more intelligent than you are. Learn from them rather than trying to teach them. Drop this stupid idea that you have to teach them. Watch them, see their authenticity, see their spontaneity, see their watchfulness, see how alert they are, how full of life and joy, how cheerful, how full of wonder and awe.

Religion arises in wonder and awe. If you can feel wonder, if you can feel awe, you are religious. Not by reading the Bible or Gita or Koran, but by experiencing awe. When you see the sky full of stars, do you feel a dance in your heart? Do you see a song arising in your being? Do you feel a communion with the stars? Then you are religious. You are not religious by going to the church or by going to the temple and repeating borrowed prayers which have nothing to do with your heart, which are just head affairs.

Religion is a love affair—a love affair with existence. And children are in that affair already. All that is needed from your side is not to destroy them. Help them to keep their wonder alive, help them to remain sincere and authentic and intelligent. But you destroy them. That's what you want, actually, by asking this question: "How can we teach . . . ?"

Religion can never be taught, it can only be caught. Are you religious? Have you the vibe of religion around you? Then you will not ask such a stupid question. Then your children will learn it just by being with you. If they see you with tears of joy watching a sunset, they are bound to be affected; they will fall silent. You need not tell them to be silent; they will see the tears and they will understand the language.

Watch the intelligence of children. And whenever you find intelligence, rejoice in it and help them and tell them, "This is the way you should go on moving."

Dad criticized the sermon, Mother thought the organist made a lot of mistakes. Sister did not like the choir's singing. But they had second thoughts when the young son piped up, "Still, it was a pretty good show for twenty pence."

The owner of a chicken farm wanted to make his son behave better, so he devised an object lesson.

"Do you see, my son? The chickens that were bad were eaten by a fox."

"So?" replied his son. "If they had been good, we would have eaten them!"

Two six-year-olds were examining an abstract painting in a gift shop. Looking at a blotch of paint, "Let's run," said one, "before they say we did it!"

A father returned home from his usual day at the office and found his small son on the front steps looking very unhappy. "What is wrong, son?" he asked.

"Just between you and me," the boy said, "I simply can't get along with your wife."

A father took his young son to an opera for the first time. The conductor started waving the baton and the soprano began her aria. The boy finally asked, "Why is he hitting her with his stick?"

"He is not hitting her, he is just waving it in the air," replied the father.

"Then why is she screaming?"

You just watch small children a little bit and you will see their intelligence.

Johnny was just home after his first day at school.

"Well, darling," asked his mother, "what did they teach you?"

"Not much," replied the child. "I have got to go again."

If you watch small children, their inventiveness, their intelligence, their constant exploration into the unknown, their curiosity, their inquiry, you need not teach them any beliefs.

Help them to understand and tell them to find their religion.

You don't allow children to vote; for political ideology they have to wait for eighteen years, then you think they are ripe enough to vote. And for religious ideology they are ripe enough when they are four or five! Do you think religious education is of lower grade than the political education? Do you think to belong to a political party needs higher intelligence, more maturity, than to belong to a religion? If eighteen years is the age for political maturity, then at least thirty-six years should be the age for religious maturity. Before thirty-six years nobody should choose any religion. Inquire, search, explore, and explore all over the place, explore in every possible direction. And when you decide your religion on your own it has significance: when it is imposed on you, it is slavery. When you choose it, it is a commitment, it is involvement.

And morality is a by-product of religion. When one feels in the heart religion arising, a relationship, a communion with existence happening, one becomes moral. It is not a question of commandments, it is not a question of shoulds and should nots; it is a question of love, compassion. When you are silent, a deep compassion arises for the whole existence, and out of that compassion one becomes moral. One cannot be cruel, one cannot kill, one cannot destroy. When you are silent, blissful, you start becoming a blessing to everybody else. That phenomenon of becoming a blessing to everybody else is true morality.

Morality has nothing to do with so-called moral principles. These so-called moral principles only create hypocrites: they create only pseudo people, split personalities. A schizophrenic humanity has come about because of thousands of priests, so-called saints and mahatmas and their continuous teachings: "Do this, don't do that." You are not helped to be aware, to see what is right and what is wrong. You are not given eyes, you are simply given directions.

My effort here is to help so that you can open your eyes—to uncover your eyes, to remove all kinds of curtains from your eyes, so that you can see what is right. And when you see what is right you are bound to do it, you cannot do otherwise. When you see what is wrong you cannot do it; it is impossible.

Religion brings clarity and clarity transforms your character.

You often tell us not to judge ourselves or other people. I am a teacher and because of my job I have to judge the students. Now I am worried about how I shall manage with my job. Can you give me some help?

My saying that you should not judge does not mean that you cannot say to a student, because you are a teacher, "The answer you have brought is not right." It is not judging the person, it is judging the act. And I am not telling you not to judge the act—that is a totally different thing.

For example, somebody is a thief—you can judge that stealing is not good. But don't judge the person, because the person is a vast phenomenon and the act is a small thing. The act is so small a piece . . . that small piece should not become a judgment about the whole person. A thief may have many beautiful values; he may be truthful, he may be sincere, he may be a very loving person.

But most often what happens is just the opposite: people start judging the person rather than the action. Actions have to be corrected—and particularly in a profession like teaching, you have to correct; you cannot allow students to go on doing wrong things. That will be very cruel, uncompassionate. But don't correct them according to tradition, convention, according to so-called morality, according to your prejudices. Whenever you are correcting somebody be very meditative, be very silent; look at the whole thing from all perspectives. Perhaps it is the right thing that they are doing, and your prevention will not be right at all.

So when I say, "Don't judge," I simply mean that no action gives you the right to condemn the person. If the action is not right, help the person. Help the person find out why the action is not right, but there is no question of judgment. Don't take the person's dignity, don't humiliate him, don't make him feel guilty—that's what I mean when I say, "Don't judge." But as far as correcting is concerned—unprejudiced, silently, in your awareness, if you see that something is wrong and will destroy that person's intelligence, will take him on the wrong paths in his life, help him.

The job of the teacher is not just to teach futile things—geography, and history, and all kinds of nonsense. The teacher's basic function is to bring the students to a better consciousness, to a higher consciousness. This should be your love and your compassion, and this should be the only value on which you judge any action as right or wrong.

But never for a single moment let the person feel that he has been condemned. On the contrary, let him feel that he has been loved—it is out of love that you have tried to correct him.

A guy lying in a hospital bed, coming around from an anesthetic, wakes up to find the doctor sitting beside him. "I have got bad news and good news for you," says the doctor, "would you like the bad or good first?"

"Aaagh," groans the guy, "tell me the bad."

"Well," says the doctor. "We had to amputate both your legs above the knee."

"Aaagh," groans the guy, "that's really bad."

After recovering from the shock, he asks the doctor for the good news.

"Well," said the doctor, "the man in the next bed would like to buy your slippers!"

Just don't be serious! Don't think that you are a teacher so you are in a very serious job. Look at life with more playful eyes . . . it is really hilarious! There is nothing to judge—everybody is doing his best. If you feel disturbed by somebody, it is your problem, not his. First correct yourself.

***I am a nursery school teacher, I teach children four and five
years old. Is there anything you can say to help me do this job as
beautifully as possible?***

To be with children is one of the most beautiful things. But one
has to learn it, otherwise it can be the most tedious thing in the
world. One has to love it, otherwise it is one of the most frustrating
things. It can drive you crazy. It can bring a nervous breakdown,
because children are so noisy, so uncivilized, uncultured . . . animals; they can drive anybody crazy! One child is enough to drive
anybody crazy, so a whole lot of children, a whole class of children
is really difficult. But if you love, it is a great discipline.

So don't only teach them—learn, too, because they still have
something which you have lost. They will also lose it sooner or
later. Before they do, learn from them. They are still spontaneous,
they are still fearless. They are still innocent. They are losing it fast.
The more civilization develops, the sooner childhood ends. Before,
it used to end somewhere near fourteen, fifteen, sixteen. Now even
a child of seven years is no longer a child. He starts becoming mature. Maturity comes sooner now because we know better methods
to condition, to structure.

So it is good, with four- and five-year-olds, to become four or five
years old. And don't think that you know and they don't know.
Listen—they know something. They know more intuitively. They are
not knowledgeable but they have a vision, a very clear vision. Their
eyes are still unclouded and their hearts are still streaming. They are
still unpolluted. The poison has not yet started. They are still natural.

So with them, don't be knowledgeable. Don't be a teacher—be
a friend. Befriend them and start looking for cues for innocence,
for spontaneity, for intelligence. You will be helped tremendously
and your meditation will go very deep.

• • •

You just have to be a caring atmosphere around them, so whatsoever they want to do you can help them to do better. Just help them to do it better. And they are not in any game, ambition game.

We are not trying to make them very powerful, famous, rich, this and that, in their life, no. Our whole effort is to help them to be alive, authentic, loving, flowing, and life takes care. A trust in life—that's what has to be created around them, so they can trust in life. Not that they have to struggle but can relax. And as for education, just help them to be more creative. Painting is good—they should try painting—or creating something else, but let it be creative; let them do things on their own. And don't bring in your criteria.

When a child paints, don't bring in adultish criteria; don't say that this is not Picasso. If the child has enjoyed it and when he was painting he got absorbed in it, that's enough. The painting is great! Not because of any objective criterion—the painting may be just nonsense; it may be just colors splashed, may be messy . . . it has to be, because a child is a child; he has a different vision of things.

For example, if a child makes the face of a man he has a different vision. He will make very big eyes; the nose will be very small. The ears may be missing—he has never looked at them—but eyes are very important for him. If he makes a man he will make the head and the hands and the legs and the torso will be missing—that is his vision. For you it is wrong but from his standpoint that is how he looks at a man: hands, legs and head. So it is not the question that you have to judge whether the painting is good or bad. No, we are not going to judge at all. Don't make the child feel good or bad about it. If the child is absorbed in painting it, that's enough. He was in deep meditation, he moved with the painting utterly . . . he was lost in it! The painting is good because the painter was lost.

Help the child to be completely lost, and whenever a child is painting on his own, he will be lost. If you force him to paint then he will be distracted. So whatsoever the children want to do, let them do; just help them. You can help in many technical ways. You can tell them how to mix colors, how to fix the canvas, how to use the brush; you can help with that. Be a help there; rather than being a guide, be a help.

Just as a gardener helps the tree . . . You cannot pull on the tree to make it grow fast; you cannot do anything in that way, nothing can be done positively. You plant the seed, you water, you give the manure, and you wait! The tree happens on its own. When the tree is happening you protect it so somebody does not hurt it or harm it. That is the function of a teacher: the teacher has to be a gardener. Not that you have to create the child; the child is coming on its own—existence is the creator.

That's what Socrates means when he says, "I am a midwife." A midwife does not create the child. The child is already there, ready to come out; the midwife helps.

So help them to be creative, help them to be joyous, because that has disappeared from the schools. Children are very sad, and sad children create a sad world. They are going to inhabit the world, and we destroy their joy. Help their joy, help their celebration, make them more and more cheerful. Nothing is more valuable than that.

Man can be saved only if society is de-schooled, or if totally different kinds of schools that cannot be called schools are evolved; only then can humanity be saved.

So no ambition should be there, no comparison ever. Never compare a child with another and say, "Look, the other has done a better painting!" That is ugly, violent, destructive. You are destroying both the children. The one you say has done a better painting starts getting the idea of the ego, superiority, and the one who has been condemned starts feeling inferior. And these are the illnesses—the superior and the inferior—so never compare!

It will be difficult for you and other teachers because comparison is so much in us. Never compare. Each child has to be respected on his own. Each child has to be respected as unique.

7

reconciliation with the parents

I am angry with my parents for the first time. My anger is so much in conflict with my love that it hurts. Can you help?

Every child would be angry if he understood what the poor parents have been doing to him unknowingly, unconsciously. All their efforts are for the good of the child. Their intentions are good but their consciousness is nil. And good intentions in the hands of unconscious people are dangerous; they cannot bring about the result they are intending. They may create just the opposite.

Every parent is trying to bring a beautiful child into the world, but looking at the world it seems it is an orphanage. There has been no parent at all. In fact if it were an orphanage, it would have been far better, because you would at least have been yourself—no parents to interfere with you.

So the anger is natural, but useless. To be angry does not help your parents and it harms you.

Gautam Buddha is reported to have made a very strange statement: In your anger you punish yourself for somebody else's fault.

It looks very strange the first time you come across the statement that in anger you punish yourself for somebody else's fault.

Your parents have done something twenty years back, thirty years back, and you are angry now. Your anger is not going to help anyone; it is simply going to create more wounds in you. I am trying to explain to you the whole mechanism of how children are being brought up. You should become more understanding that whatever has happened had to happen. Your parents were conditioned by their parents. You cannot find out who was really responsible to be-gin with. It has been passed from generation to generation.

Your parents are doing exactly what has been done to them. They have been victims. You will feel compassion for them and you will feel joyous that you are not going to repeat the same thing in your life. If you decide to have children you will feel joyous that you are going to break the vicious circle, that you can become the dead end. You will not do it to your children or to any other person's children.

You should feel fortunate that you have a master with you to explain what has been happening between parents and children—the complex upbringing, good intentions, bad results, where every-body is trying to do the best and the world goes on becoming worse and worse. Your parents were not so fortunate to have a master—and you are being angry at them. You should feel kind, compassionate, loving. Whatever they did was unconscious. They could not have done otherwise. All that they knew they have tried on you. They were miserable, and they have created another miser-able human being in the world.

They had no clarity about why they were miserable. You have the clarity to understand why one becomes miserable. And once you understand how misery is created, you can avoid causing the same in somebody else.

But feel for your parents. They worked hard; they did everything they could, but they had no idea how psychology functions. Instead of being taught how to become a mother or how to become a father, they were being taught how to become a Christian, how to become a Marxist, how to become a tailor, how to become a plumber, how to become a philosopher—all these things are good and needed, but the basic thing is missing. If they are going to produce children, then their most significant teaching should be how to become a mother, how to become a father.

It has been taken for granted that by giving birth you know how to become a mother and how to become a father. Yes, as far as giving birth to a child . . . it is a biological act, you don't have to be psychologically trained for it. Animals are doing perfectly well, birds are doing perfectly well, trees are doing perfectly well. But giving birth to a child biologically is one thing and to be a mother or to be a father is totally different. It needs great education because you are creating a human being.

Animals are not creating anything, they are simply producing carbon copies. And now science has come to a point where they have discovered that carbon copies can really be produced! It is a very dangerous idea. If we make gene banks—and sooner or later we are going to make them; once an idea is there it is going to become a reality. And scientifically it is proved that it is 100 percent possible . . . there is no problem. We can have banks in the hospitals for both the male sperms and female eggs. And we can create exactly the same two sperms and exactly the same two eggs, so two children are born which are exactly the same. One child will be released into the world; the other will grow in a fridge, unconscious, but all his parts will be exactly the same as the other person. And if the first person is in an accident and loses a leg or loses a kidney, or has to be operated on, there is no problem: his carbon copy is waiting in the hospital. From the carbon copy a kidney can be taken out—he is growing exactly at the same rate, he is just unconscious—and it will be exactly the same as the kidney that has been lost. It can be replaced.

This idea of having carbon copies seems to be a great advancement in medical science in a way, but it is dangerous—dangerous in the sense that man becomes a machine with replaceable parts, just like any machine. When something goes wrong you replace the part. And if every part can be replaced, then man will be falling further and further away from spiritual growth because he will start thinking of himself as just a machine. That's what half of the world, the communist world, thinks—that man is a machine.

You are fortunate that you can understand the situation your parents were in. They have not done anything specifically to you; they would have done the same to any child that was born to them. They were programmed for that. They were helpless. And to be angry against helpless people is simply not right. It is unjust, unfair, and moreover it is harmful to you.

You can help them by really becoming the individual that I am talking about: more conscious, more alert, more loving. Seeing you can only change them. Seeing you so radically changed can only make them think twice, that perhaps they are wrong. There is no other way. You cannot intellectually convince them. Intellectually they can argue, and argument never changes anybody. The only thing that changes people is the charisma, the magnetism, the magic, of your individuality. Then whatever you touch becomes golden.

So rather than wasting your time and energy in being angry and fighting against the past, which no longer exists, put your whole energy into becoming the magic of your individuality. So when your parents see you they cannot remain untouched by the new qualities that you have grown, qualities that are automatically impressive: your freshness, your understanding, your unconditional lovingness, your kindness even in a situation where anger would have been more appropriate.

Only these things can be the real arguments. You need not say a word. Your eyes, your face, your actions, your behavior, your response, will make the change in them. They will start inquiring about what has happened to you, how it has happened to you—because everybody wants these qualities. These are the real riches. Nobody is so rich that he can afford not to have the things that I am telling you.

So put your energy into transforming yourself. That will help you, and that will help your parents. Perhaps it may create a chain reaction. Your parents may have other children, they may have friends, and it will go on and on. It is just like you are sitting on the bank of a silent lake and you throw a small pebble into the lake. The pebble is so small that it creates a small circle at first, but circle after circle . . . and they go on spreading to the far ends, as far as the lake can take them. And it was only a small pebble.

We are living in a certain kind of new sphere, a new psychological lake, in which whatever you do creates certain vibrations around you. It touches people, reaches to unknown sources. Just create a small ripple of right individuality and it will reach to many people—and certainly to those who are most closely related to you. They will see it first, and they will understand with great awe. So feel blissful. You have a chance to get totally transformed. And help your parents, because they did not have such a chance; feel sorry for them.

My parents are so disappointed in me, they worry all the time. What do I owe to my parents?

The trouble with the family is that children grow out of childhood, but parents never grow out of their parenthood! Man has not even yet learned that parenthood is not something that you have to cling to forever. When the child is a grown-up person your parenthood is finished. The child needed it—he was helpless. He needed the mother, the father, their protection; but when the child can stand on his own, the parents have to learn how to withdraw from the life of the child. And because parents never withdraw from the life of the child, they remain a constant anxiety to themselves and to the children. They destroy, they create guilt; they don't help beyond a certain limit.

To be a parent is a great art; very few people are really capable of being parents.

Don't be worried at all—all parents are disappointed in their children! And I say all, without any exception. Even the parents of Gautam Buddha were very much disappointed in him, the parents of Jesus Christ were very much disappointed in him, obviously. They had lived a certain kind of life—they were orthodox Jews— and this son, this Jesus, was going against many traditional ideas, conventions. Jesus's father, Joseph, must have hoped that now when he is growing old the son will help him in his carpentry, in his work, in his shop—and the stupid son started talking about kingdom of God! Do you think he was very happy in his old age?

Gautam Buddha's father was old and he had only one son, and that too was born to him when he was very old. His whole life he has waited and prayed and worshipped and has done all kinds of religious rituals so that he could have a son, because who is going to look after his great kingdom? Then one day the son disappeared from the palace! Do you think he was happy? He was so angry, violently angry, he would have killed Gautam Buddha if he had found him! His police, his detectives were searching all over the kingdom. "Where he is hiding? Bring him to me!"

And Buddha knew it, that he would be caught by his father's agents, so the first thing he did was to leave the boundary of his father's kingdom; he escaped into another kingdom and for twelve years nothing was heard about him.

When he became enlightened he came back home to share his

joy, to say to the father that "I have arrived home," that "I have realized," that "I have known the truth—and this is the way." But the father was so angry, he was trembling and shaking—he was old, very old. He shouted at Buddha and he said, "You are a disgrace to me!" He saw Buddha—he was standing there in a beggar's robe with a begging bowl—and he said, "How do you dare to stand before me like a beggar? You are the son of an emperor, and in our family there has never been a beggar! My father was an emperor, his father was too, and for centuries we have been emperors! You have disgraced the whole heritage!"

Buddha listened for half an hour, he didn't say a single word. When the father ran out of gas, cooled down a little . . . tears were coming out of his eyes, tears of anger, frustration. Then Buddha said, "I ask for only one favor. Please wipe your tears and look at me—I am not the same person who had left home, I am totally transformed. But your eyes are so full of tears you cannot see. You are still talking to somebody who is no more! He has died."

This triggered another outburst of anger, and the father said, "You are trying to teach me? Do you think I am a fool? Can't I recognize my own son? My blood is running in your veins—and I cannot recognize you?"

Buddha said, "Please don't misunderstand me. The body certainly belongs to you, but not my consciousness. And my consciousness is my reality, not my body. You are right that your father was an emperor and his father too, but as far as I know about myself I was a beggar in my past life and I was a beggar in a previous life too, because I have been searching for truth. My body has come through you, but you have been just like a passage. You have not created me; you have been a medium, and my consciousness has nothing to do with your consciousness. What I am saying is that now I have come home with a new consciousness, I have gone through a rebirth. Just look at me, look at my joy!"

And the father looked at the son, not believing what he was saying. But one thing was certainly true: he was so angry, but the son had not reacted at all. That was absolutely new—he knew his son. If he was just the old person he would have become as angry as the father or even more, because he was young and his blood was hotter than the father's. But he was not angry at all, there was absolute peace on his face, a great silence. He was undisturbed, undistracted by the father's anger. The father has abused him, but it seems not to have affected him at all.

He wiped his tears from the old eyes, looked again, saw the new grace. . . .

Your parents will be disappointed in you because they must have been trying to fulfill some expectations through you. But don't become guilty because of it, otherwise they will destroy your joy, your silence, your growth. You remain undisturbed, unworried. Don't feel any guilt. Your life is yours and you have to live according to your own light.

And when you have arrived at the source of joy, your inner bliss, go to them to share. They will be angry—wait, because anger is not anything permanent; it comes like a cloud and passes. Wait! Go there, be with them, but only when you are certain that you can still remain cool, only when you know that nothing will create any reaction in you, only when you know that you will be able to respond with love even though they are angry. That will be the only way to help them.

You say: *They worry all the time.*

That is their business! And don't think that if you had followed their ideas they would not have worried. They would have still worried; that is their conditioning. Their parents must have worried and their parents' parents must have worried; that is their heritage. And you have disappointed them because you are no longer worrying. You are going astray! They are miserable, their parents have been miserable, and so on, so forth . . . back to Adam and Eve! And you are going astray, hence the great worry.

But if you become worried you miss an opportunity, and then they have dragged you again back into the same mire. They will feel good, they will rejoice that you have come back to the old traditional, conventional way, but that is not going to help you or them.

If you remain independent, if you attain to the fragrance of freedom, if you become more meditative—and that's why you are here, to become more meditative, to be more silent, more loving, more blissful—then one day you can share your bliss. To share first you have to have it; you can share only that which you have already.

Right now you can also worry, but two persons worrying simply multiply worries; they don't help each other.

It must have been their conditioning. It is the conditioning of everybody in the world.

A rabbi was being hosted by a family, and the man of the house, impressed by the honor, warned his children to behave seriously at the dinner table because the great rabbi is coming. But during the course of the meal they laughed at something and he ordered them from the table.

The rabbi immediately arose and prepared to leave.

"Anything wrong?" asked the concerned father.

"Well," said the rabbi, "I laughed too!"

Don't be worried about their seriousness, about their worrying about you. They are trying unconsciously to make you feel guilty. Don't let them succeed, because if they succeed they will destroy you and they will also destroy an opportunity for themselves which would have become possible through you.

You say: *What do I owe my parents?*

You owe this: that you have to be yourself. You owe this: that you have to be blissful, that you have to be ecstatic, that you have to become a celebration unto yourself, that you have to learn to laugh and rejoice. They have helped you physically, you have to help them spiritually. That will be the only way to repay them.

I feel guilty about my mother. I can't give her love, attention, and since she is living in the same house it has become worse and I don't know what to do with her.

A few things. First: mothers, fathers, demand too much, more than is possible for the children to give, because the natural course is that they love you because you are their children. But you cannot love them in the same way, because they are not your children. You will love your children, and the same will happen again: your children will not be able to love you in the same way, because the river moves onward, not backward. The natural course is that the parents will love the children and the children will love their children; it cannot move backward. But the demand seems to be natural. Because the mother has loved you, she thinks you should love her in the same way. And the more she demands, the less you will be capable of returning the love, and the more she will create a feeling of guilt in you. So drop that idea—completely drop it; it is natural. You cannot love her in the same way that she has loved you, and nothing is wrong with you, nothing at all. That's how it happens to every child; that's how nature intends it to happen.

If children love their parents too much they will not be able to love their own children. That will be more dangerous—then the survival of the species will be at risk. Your mother has also not loved her mother. At the most one can be polite, formal, but love does not flow backward. One can be respectful, that's true—one should be respectful, but love is not possible. Once you understand that love is not possible the guilt feeling will disappear.

There are a few people who become too attached, too obsessed with their parents; they are psychologically ill. If a woman loves the mother too much she will not be able to love a man because she will always find that her mother will suffer, that it will be creating a kind of conflict. If she loves a man her love will flow toward that man and she will feel guilty. They will never enjoy life and they will be angry also at their parents. Deep down they will hope, "Someday if the mother dies or if the father dies, then I will be free," although they will not tell it to anybody—not even to themselves will they tell it. It will just be there lurking in their unconscious, because that seems to be the only possibility to be free. That's not good—to think of your parents as dead—but that's how it happens if you become too attached.

There is no need—just be respectful, that's all. Take care, whatsoever you can do, do, but don't feel guilt at all. And if parents are understanding they will understand this. This happens in animals—in animals there is no question: the moment the child is able to stand on his or her own, the child leaves the parents. The parents don't go after the child saying, "Listen, where are you going? We have done so much for you. . . ." That is not asked in nature at all.

And it is not that the mother and father have not done anything; they have done much—particularly the mother has done much, but it was her joy. To carry you in her womb was her joy. To nourish you, to bring you up, was her joy. She has been rewarded already. Nothing more is needed to be given to her; there is no question of giving. She enjoyed those moments—when she was pregnant she enjoyed it. When she gave birth she was happy because she became a mother, she was fulfilled. Then she brought you up and she was happy: she is bringing up a child . . . a natural happiness. She has been rewarded already. Nature always rewards immediately; it never keeps files hanging.

So don't feel guilty—that's where you have to change your mind. Drop the guilt and then see the change coming.

There is no need, if you don't feel good, to go to her. Go only when you feel good! Never go because of any duty. Never go because you have to. Only go when you feel really happy and you would like to be with your mother for a few moments. It is better to be happy and there only for a few moments rather than to be horrible and be there for hours and create misery for her and yourself. Be a little more aware.

I have a knot in my stomach at the idea of seeing my parents. I either become very distant, mechanical with them, or very argumentative and defensive. I don't have the compassion for them. Should I go into therapy?

There is no need. It is just a fear which comes from the past. Your energy is perfectly good: there is no knot in the energy, the knot is just in your memory. These are two different things.

If the knot is in the energy then it is a difficult thing. But if the knot is just in the memory it is a very simple thing, you can drop it just like that. My suggestion is that before going into anything else, just be happy for two, three months. Just enjoy life with no barrier, with no guilt, with no inhibition. If you can enjoy life with no guilt and no inhibition, a great compassion for your parents will arise in you.

In fact, no child is ever able to forgive his parents unless he becomes guiltless, because parents mean guilt. They have created the basic guilt: do this, don't do that; be like this and don't be like that. They were the first creative elements, but they were also destructive. They helped the child to grow, they loved the child, but they had their own minds and conditionings and they tried to impose those conditionings on the child. So every child hates the parents.

You are feeling against your parents, afraid of your parents because they don't allow you to be yourself. So whenever they are there, you start feeling cramps, you feel knots in your stomach, because they won't allow you to be yourself. Again you become a child in their presence; again the past becomes alive. Again you are helpless, and you are not a child now, so naturally you become argumentative, you retaliate, you become angry or you become very defensive, or you start avoiding . . . but all these things create a distance.

And there is a deep urge in you to love your parents; that's so with everybody. You have come from them, you owe your life to them. Everybody loves this origin but the origin has done something which does not allow closeness, communication, so when you come close there is a problem. If you don't come close, some deep urge to commune, to forgive, to make new bridges is there.

For three months just live as you would like to, and that will be the cleaning of this memory part. Just live the way you want to live. Your parents are not obstructing you anymore. Your parents will speak from within you many times: you will be doing something and a parental voice will come, "Don't do this." Laugh at that parental voice and remember that now you are free and your parents have made you mature enough that you can live your own life and can take responsibility for it. So no need for this voice—now you have your own consciousness, you need not have a substitute for it. Now the parents need not speak for you; you can speak on your own.

For three months try this; within three months this knot will disappear. It can be washed away very easily, it can be erased. And you can do it on your own, then there is no need for therapy. If you cannot and you feel it is difficult, then therapy will be helpful. It will do the same thing: it will try to erase the memory. If you cannot do it alone it is always good to take the support of any expert who knows how to do it, but first try it on your own.

Otherwise, what happens sometimes is that your therapist may be able to help you to get rid of your parents but he becomes your parent. The mind is so clumsy, so confused, that if it starts losing some grip on something, it immediately starts grabbing something else from some other direction as a substitute. So, many people who go to the therapist by and by get rid of many problems but then the therapist becomes the problem. Then they cannot afford to lose the therapist; they cannot drop out of therapy. They can change the therapist, they can change the therapy, they can go from one kind of therapy to another kind of therapy, but they become therapy addicts.

It is very good sometimes to tackle your problems on your own—it will give you more confidence.

And this is the process—to do whatsoever you want to do. Good or bad, that is not the point. Whatsoever you want to do is good for these three months, and whatsoever you don't want to do is bad, so don't do it. Be completely at ease and free, and enjoy life almost as if you are born for the first time. And that's exactly what is happening through sannyas. You are a new child, it is a new birth. You can start growing along a new line, and then those parental voices and the parental conditioning will not come in the way at all; it is a new growth.

My father suddenly died and I feel I have to go somehow to be with my mother, to finish something there. There is something that feels so unfinished emotionally with her, and now seems the time.

It is always so with parents. The relationship is such that to finish it needs great awareness—only then can it be finished. Even the idea to finish it may not allow it to finish. So don't carry that idea. Just be there . . . naturally there, lovingly there. Do whatsoever you can do—because parents have done much, and in the West they are not even thanked for it. Nobody feels any gratitude.

In the East it has been totally different. In the East it is never an unfinished situation. It is always complete, because parents have given so much and children have always been giving as much reverence as possible, as much respect as possible. That has become so natural in the East, and it has to be so for a very deep reason.

If you are not in rapport with your patents you will not be in rapport with yourself, because parents are not just an accidental phenomenon—they are deeply in your roots . . . you come from them. Half of your being comes from your mother, half of your being comes from your father. They both will carry on in you. All their conflict will continue in you . . . all their anxieties will deep down continue. It is for your sake that you have to come to a rapport. And the easiest way is not to make any effort for it.

Effort will never help—it is very artificial. So drop this idea, otherwise you will come back feeling again that something has remained incomplete.

Just go there, be there. And she will need you in this moment. When your father is gone she will be in a great sorrow—she will need you. So don't make any effort deliberately. Just be with her, caress her, care about her . . . sometimes meditate with her, help her to meditate if she can. Otherwise just tell her that you will meditate in her room; she can simply rest in her bed and you will meditate. That very vibration will help her.

Be happy. It will be difficult in a situation, in this situation, but still be happy. Take cheerfulness for her . . . make the burden light. Help her to accept the situation.

And don't bother about your relationship, and suddenly you will see that it is healed. It is indirect—you cannot work directly. And if for two, three weeks you can be very loving and helping and she feels happy that you have come—she feels happy that you have some totally different kind of energy that she needed, that you have been a nourishment to her—that's enough. You will feel a rapport coming.

If we can be loving, no relationship remains hanging. Each moment it has a completion. ˙

I am suspicious about my father. I don't think he is my real father. Can you help me get rid of this doubt?

This is a really difficult question! In the first place, it matters not. It is irrelevant whether A is your father or B is your father. How does it matter? You are you, you are that which you are. From where your first cell came, from where, from what source, makes no difference now.

Why are you so worried about it? But such things sometimes become obsessions. Even if you come to know, even if I say that "This man is your father"—for example, if I say Paul is your father, then what? Are you going to believe me? Then you will start doubting me, so it is better that you doubt your father! Or you may start doubting poor Paul, who has nothing to do with it!

Only your mother can answer. Even your father cannot answer, because even your father may not be right. Ask your mother.

A youngster went to his father and said, "Dad, I would like to marry Susy." "Don't marry her, son," said the old man. "When I was a kid I sowed my wild oats, and well, you know how it is."

About a week later the boy came to his father again and

said, "Dad, I am in love with Mildred and I want to marry her."

The old salesman said, "She is your half-sister, son. You can't marry her."

"How about Mabel?" the kid asked a couple of weeks later.

"She is your half-sister too," said Dad.

The youngster, who was anxious to get married, went to his mom and complained, "Pop says I should not marry Susy, Mildred, or Mabel because they are my half-sisters. What do I do?"

Mom put her arms around her boy and consoled, "You can marry any one of them you like—he is not your father!"

So it is a very difficult thing unless your mother is truthful about it; nobody can give you a guarantee.

I have heard about one machine that IBM has produced. I don't know whether it is true or not, but you can inquire.

A woman, having heard how fantastic the IBM machines are, enters the IBM salesroom to look around.

"You can ask the machine any question you like and it will give you the correct answer," explains the salesman.

The woman writes the question, "Where is my father?" and puts it into the machine. The answer comes back, "Your father is fishing off the west coast of Florida."

"Ridiculous!" exclaims the woman. "My father has been dead twenty years."

"The machine never makes a mistake," the salesman proclaims. "There is simply a misunderstanding. Rephrase your question and ask it again."

The woman writes down for the machine, "Where is my mother's husband?"

The IBM machine answers, "He has been dead twenty years, but your father is fishing off the west coast of Florida."

But please don't ask such questions of me, I am not an IBM machine—neither am I your mother!

8

meditation

Meditation is a natural state—which we have lost. It is a paradise lost, but the paradise can be regained. Look into the child's eyes, look and you will see tremendous silence, innocence. Each child comes with a meditative state, but he has to be initiated into the ways of the society—he has to be taught how to think, how to calculate, how to reason, how to argue; he has to be taught words, language, concepts. And, slowly slowly, he loses contact with his own innocence. He becomes contaminated, polluted by the society. He becomes an efficient mechanism; he is no more a man.

All that is needed is to regain that space once more. You had known it before, so when for the first time you know meditation, you will be surprised—because a great feeling will arise in you as if you have known it before. And that feeling is true: you have known it before. You have forgotten. The diamond is lost in piles of rubbish. But if you can uncover it, you will find the diamond again—it is yours.

It cannot really be lost: it can only be forgotten. We are born as meditators, then we learn the ways of the mind. But our real nature remains hidden somewhere deep down like an undercurrent. Any day, a little digging, and you will find the source still flowing, the source of fresh waters. And the greatest joy in life is to find it.

Surely, meditation is for mystics. Why do you propose it for ordinary people and their children?

It is for mystics, surely, but everybody is a born mystic—because everybody carries a great mystery within him that has to be realized; everybody carries great potentiality that has to be actualized. Everybody is born with a future. Everybody has hope.

What do you mean by a mystic? A mystic is one who is trying to realize the mystery of life, who is moving into the unknown, who is going into the uncharted, whose life is a life of adventure, exploration. Every child starts that way—with awe, with wonder, with great inquiry in his heart. Every child is a mystic. Somewhere on the way of your so-called growing you lose contact with your inner possibility of being a mystic. You become a businessman or you become a clerk, or you become a civil servant or you become a minister. You become something else and you start thinking that you are this. And when you believe it, it is so.

My effort here is to destroy your wrong notions about yourself and to liberate your mysticism. Meditation is a way of liberating the mysticism, and it is for everybody—without any exception, it knows no exception.

And children are the most capable. They are natural mystics. Before they are destroyed by the society, before they are destroyed by other robots, by other corrupted people, it is better to help them to know something of meditation.

Meditation is not a conditioning because meditation is not indoctrination. Meditation is not giving them any creed. If you teach a child to become Christian you have to give him a doctrine; you have to force him to believe things which naturally look absurd. You have to tell the child that Jesus was born out of a virgin mother—that becomes a fundamental. Now you are destroying the natural intelligence of the child. But if you teach a child meditation you are not indoctrinating him. You don't say he has to believe anything, you simply invite him to an experiment in no-thought. No-thought is not a doctrine, it is an experience. And children are very, very capable because they are very close to the source. They still remember something of that mystery. They have just come from the other world, they have not yet forgotten it completely. Sooner or later they will forget, but still the fragrance is around them. That's why all children look so beautiful, so graceful.

Have you even seen an ugly child? Then what happens to all these beautiful children? Where do they disappear to? Later in life it is very rare to find beautiful people. So what happens to all the beautiful children, why do they turn into ugly persons? What accident, what calamity happens on the way?

They start losing their grace the day they start losing their intelligence. They start losing their natural rhythm, their natural elegance and they start learning plastic behavior. They no longer laugh spontaneously, they no longer cry spontaneously, they no longer dance spontaneously. You have forced them into a cage, a straitjacket. You have imprisoned them. The chains are very subtle, they are not very visible. The chains are of thought—Christian, Hindu, Mohammedan. You have chained the child and he cannot see the chains, so he will not be able to see how he is chained. And he will suffer his whole life. It is such an imprisonment. It is not like throwing a person into a jail. It is creating a jail around a person, so wherever he goes the jail continues around him. He can go to the Himalayas and sit in a cave and he will remain a Hindu, he will remain a Christian—and he will still think thoughts.

Meditation is a way to go within yourselves to that depth where thoughts don't exist. So it is not indoctrination. It is not teaching you anything, in fact; it is just making you alert to your inner capacity to be without thought, to be without mind. And the best time is when the child is still uncorrupted.

A curious thing happened to me when I was a little girl—perhaps eleven or twelve years old. During recess time at school I was in the bathroom and looked into the mirror to see if I looked tidy. Then suddenly I found that I was standing halfway between my body and the mirror, watching myself looking at my reflection in the mirror. It amused me to see the three I's, and I thought it must have been a trick one could learn. So I tried to show my girlfriend and I tried it again myself—without success.

It felt like my essential self had stepped out of my physical form. Is it of any value to understand what happened to that little girl?

It happens to many children, but because the atmosphere around is not supportive of awareness, those experiences are not nourished by the parents, the school, the friends, the teachers. And if you say that it has happened to you, people will laugh—and you yourself will think that something has gone wrong, that it was not right.

For example, all children in every culture around the world like to whirl. And every parent stops them from whirling and says, "You will fall down." It is true, there is a possibility they may fall down. But that falling down is not going to harm them much. Why do children like whirling? While the body is whirling, small children can see it whirling. They are no longer identified with it, because it is such a new experience.

With everything they are identified—with walking they are identified, with eating they are identified, with anything they are doing, usually they are identified. This whirling is such an experience that the faster the body moves, whirls, the less is the possibility of their remaining identified. Soon they are lagging behind; the body is whirling but their being cannot whirl. It stops at a point and starts seeing its own body whirling. Sometimes it can come out of the body too. If the whirling child is not staying at one place but goes on moving—whirling and moving around the place—then his essential self can come out and watch it.

Such activities should be helped, nourished, and the child should be asked, "What are you experiencing?" and told, "This experience is one of the greatest in life, so don't forget it. Even if you fall, there is no harm; there is not much that can be harmful. But what you can gain is invaluable." But they are being stopped in this and in many other things.

My own experience in childhood was . . . the river of my town used to flood. Nobody used to cross it by swimming when it was flooded. It was a river that came from the mountains and ordinarily, it was small, but in rainy times it was at least a mile wide. The current of the water was tremendous; you could not stand in it. And the water was deep, so there was no way to stand anyway.

I loved it. I waited for the rainy season because it always helped . . . there would come a moment when I would feel that I was dying, because I was tired and I could not see the other shore, and the waves were high and the current was strong . . . and there was no way to go back, because now the other shore was as far away. Perhaps I was in the middle; it was the same either way. I would feel so completely tired and the water would take me down with such a force that there would come a time when I would see, "Now there is no possibility of living anymore." And that was the moment when I would suddenly see myself above the water and my body in the water. When it happened the first time, it was a very frightening experience. I thought I must have died. I had heard that when you die, the soul goes out of the body: "So I have gone out of the body and I am dead." But I could see the body was still trying to reach the other shore, so I followed the body.

That was the first time I became aware of a connection between your essential being and the body. It is connected just below the navel—two inches below the navel—by something like a silver cord, a silver rope. It is not material, but it shines like silver. Each time I reached the other shore, the moment I reached the other shore my being would enter into the body. The first time it was frightening; then it became a great entertainment.

When I told my parents, they said, "Someday you are going to die in that river. This is enough of a sign. Stop going into the river when it is flooded."

But I said, "I am enjoying it so much . . . the freedom, no force of gravitation, and seeing one's own body completely separate."

What happened to you was just accidental. If you had pursued it, it would have come back. But it was good . . . it happens to many children. But nobody persists, so once in a while it happens and then one forgets it, or one thinks perhaps one imagined it; perhaps it was something, just a fantasy, a dream. But it is a reality. You had walked out of yourself and what you saw is a kind of awareness outside the body.

What is an easy way for children to start meditation?

Children can go into meditation very easily—one just has to know how to help them toward it. They cannot be coerced; that's impossible. Nobody can ever be coerced into meditation, because coercion is violence. How can one coerce meditation? It comes when it comes. But you can persuade. You can just invite the child with tremendous respect. Dance with him, sing with him, sit in silence with him. By and by he will start imbibing it. By and by he will start enjoying the play of it. It cannot be work for the child, it cannot be serious—it should not be for anybody! It can only be a play. So help the child to play meditation. Let it be a game. Make it a game with him, and by and by he will start loving it. He will start asking you, "When are we going to play meditation?" And once he starts learning some ways of silence, then meditation has started working on him and one day you will see that he is deeper in meditation than you had ever expected. So you have to make a meditative atmosphere.

And this is my observation—that if grown-ups are a little more meditative, children imbibe the spirit very easily. They are so sensitive. They learn whatsoever is there in the atmosphere; they learn the vibe of it.

They never bother about what you say. What you *are*—they always respect that. And they have a very deep perceptivity, a clarity, an intuitiveness.

Love him and allow him to be a little meditative, and much is possible.

• • •

Society can be transformed totally if small children start meditating. They are not serious so they are very ready for meditation. They are joyful, playful. They take everything in fun. Sometimes it happens that when I tell a child, "Close your eyes" he closes the eyes and he enjoys it as nobody else enjoys it. The very idea that he has been taken so seriously rejoices him. He sits silently. Sometimes I have seen grown-up people looking, just opening their eyes a little to see what is happening. But small children, when they close their eyes, they *really* close them. They close them very hard because they are afraid they will open if they don't do it hard. They really do it hard. They bring their total energy there because they know that if they are not doing it totally then the eyes will open and they will start looking to see what the matter is, what is going on. I have seen them really closing their eyes. And to see a child sitting silently is one of the most beautiful things you can come across.

Children can be taught meditation more easily because they are not yet spoiled. When you have been spoiled the hard work is to help you to unlearn.

I have heard that whenever anybody came to Mozart, the great composer and musician, he would ask, "Have you learned music anywhere else before?" If the person had, then Mozart would ask double fees. If the person had not learned music at all then he would say, "That is okay. Even half the fee will do."

People were very puzzled because this was illogical—"When a fresh man comes, who has not known anything about music, you say half the fee, and when somebody who has been working for ten years comes you say double the fee?" Mozart said, "There is a reason. First I have to clean the slate. That is the harder work. To destroy all that the person is carrying is harder than to teach."

Teaching is very easy if you are available. With a virgin heart, teaching is very simple—and a child is a virgin heart.

I am twelve years old; can I start meditating?

This is the right age when you should start meditating, just when you are coming closer to your fourteenth year. You are twelve; these two years will be of immense value to you. After each seven years the mind changes. The fourteenth year will be one of great change, so if one is ready much becomes possible; if one is not ready then one goes on missing the change. And all that is beautiful always happens when you are passing that period of change.

So start meditating. And by meditation I mean that whenever you are sitting silently, start swaying just like you did right now. Feel like a tree and sway. As you sway and as you feel like a tree, you will disappear as a human being, in that disappearance is meditation. There are a thousand and one ways to disappear. I am giving you the most simple one that you can do very easily. Dance, and disappear into the dance; whirl, and disappear into the whirl. Jog, run, and disappear into the jogging: let the jogging be there and forget about yourself. That forgetfulness is meditation, and that is possible at this age.

Then there are different doors to meditation which become possible later on. But to a child, forgetfulness is meditation. So forget yourself in anything and you will find meditation coming to you.

• • •

Children can enter into meditation through dance very easily, because dance is not anything unnatural, artificial; man is born with the faculty of dance. Because we have stopped dancing naturally, the body is suffering very much. There are a few things that can happen only through dance: flow is possible only through dance. So help your child to participate in dancing meditations. If he can get into dance, meditation will happen of its own accord.

I'm a teacher and my children at school sometimes like to make noise and run and I do not want to force them anymore to stay still and to keep silent.

Do one thing: every day, at least twice, give them fifteen or twenty minutes to go berserk, to go completely mad and do whatsoever they want to do—to jump and scream and shout . . . just twenty minutes in the morning before you start your class. You also participate, then they will enjoy it very much—also shout and jump and participate, then they will be really into it. The moment they see that their teacher is into it, they will simply enjoy the whole trip. Just fifteen minutes will do. Tell them to be as noisy as they can and do whatsoever they want to do. Then tell them to stop and for five minutes remain silent; this will be a great meditation to them.

And if you feel it works, then once more somewhere in the afternoon before they leave, do it again. And within two or three months you will see such a change coming to the children . . . unbelievable.

Their pent-up energy has to be released. In fact they have so much energy and we are forcing them to sit and they cannot, so they are boiling! They find any chance and they will start doing mischief.

Just allow them. It will be a great help, and you will see: their intelligence will become better, their concentration will become better, their hearing capacity will become better, their understanding will become better, because they will be no longer burdened. Their love and their respect for you will increase tremendously, and then they will listen to you—and there will be no need to force them: just your saying will be enough.

You can say to them, "Wait! Soon your period for being mischievous is coming. Just wait one hour more!" They will understand that you are not prohibiting them forever. They will soon learn the rule—that there are times when they can be mischievous, noisy, and do whatsoever they want, and then of course there is time to read and study.

If some problem arises with the school authorities, talk to them, and by and by tell them. They will also be very much helped; other classes will also be helped. Just tell them that this is an experiment, and to allow you to do it for six months. Then they can come and see what has happened to the children—whether their reports are better, whether their intelligence has grown, whether their understanding is deeper. Tell them to watch, and then if they feel it is good, this can become the thing for the whole school. The whole school can gather for twenty minutes twice each day, and it will be great joy.

9

meditation techniques

GIBBERISH MEDITATION

This is a cathartic technique, which encourages expressive body movements.

Either alone or in a group, close your eyes and begin to say nonsense sounds—gibberish. The word *gibberish* comes from a Sufi mystic, Jabbar. Jabbar never spoke any language, he just uttered nonsense. Still he had thousands of disciples because what he was saying was, "Your mind is nothing but gibberish. Put it aside and you will have a taste of your own being."

To use gibberish, don't say things which are meaningful, don't use the language that you know. Use Chinese if you don't know Chinese. Use Japanese if you don't know Japanese. Don't use German if you know German. For the first time have a freedom—the same as all the birds have. Simply allow whatever comes to your mind without bothering about its rationality, reasonability, meaning, significance —just the way the birds are doing.

FIRST STAGE: 15 MINUTES

Move totally in the gibberish. Make any sounds you like, but do not speak in a language. Allow yourself to express whatever needs to be expressed within you. Throw it out. Go crazy, with absolute awareness so that you become the center of the cyclone.

The mind thinks, always, in terms of words. Gibberish helps to break up this pattern of continual verbalization. Without suppressing your thoughts, you can throw them out—in gibberish. Let your body likewise be expressive.

SECOND STAGE: 15 MINUTES

Lie down on your stomach and feel as if you are merging with mother earth. With each exhalation, feel yourself merging into the ground beneath you.

OSHO BORN AGAIN MEDITATION

This meditation lasting two hours a day for seven days can be done alone or in a group.

Be playful. It will be difficult, because you are so structured. You have an armor around you and it is so difficult to loosen it, to relax it.

Put aside knowledge, put aside seriousness; be absolutely playful for these days. You have nothing to lose. If you do not gain anything, you will not lose anything either. What can you lose in being playful? But I say to you: you will never be the same again.

In these days I want to throw you back to the point where you started being "good" as against being natural. Be playful so your childhood is regained. It will be difficult because you will have to put aside your masks, your faces; you will have to put aside your personality. But remember, the essence can assert itself only when your personality is not there, because your personality has become an imprisonment. Put it aside.

Regain your childhood. Everyone longs for it but no one is doing anything to regain it. Everyone longs for it! People go on saying that childhood is paradise and poets go on writing poems about the beauty of childhood. Who is preventing you from regaining it? I give you this opportunity to regain it.

FIRST STAGE: ONE HOUR

You behave like a child. Just enter into your childhood. Whatever you wanted to do—do it—dancing, singing, jumping, crying, weeping, anything at all in any posture. Nothing is prohibited except touching and interfering with other people.

SECOND STAGE: ONE HOUR

Sit silently in meditation. You will be more fresh, more innocent, and meditation will become easier.

MEDITATION FOR CHILDREN UP TO TWELVE YEARS

This is a meditation for children and their teachers to do together at the beginning of each school day. But it should not be made compulsory.

FIRST STAGE

Five minutes gibberish. The children should be given total freedom to shout, scream, and express their feelings.

SECOND STAGE

Five minutes laughing. They should be allowed to laugh totally. By this their minds will be more pure and fresh.

THIRD STAGE

After gibberish and laughter they should lie down for five minutes—still and silent as if they are dead, only the breathing comes and goes.

MEDITATION FOR CHILDREN OVER TWELVE YEARS

Later Osho added a further step for teenagers, introducing a five-minute crying period after the laughter and before the silence for children over twelve years.

5 minutes gibberish
5 minutes laughter
5 minutes crying
5 minutes lying down as if dead

Move back into the womb

Before you go to sleep, sit in your bed—sit in a relaxed way and close your eyes. Feel the body relaxing . . . If the body starts leaning forward allow it; it may lean forward. It may like to take a womb posture—just as when a child is in the mother's womb. If you feel like that, move into the womb posture, become a small child in the mother's womb.

Then just listen to your breathing, nothing else. Just listen to it—the breathing going in, the breathing going out. I am not saying to say it—just feel it going in; when it is going out, feel it going out. And in that feeling you feel tremendous silence and clarity arising.

This is just for ten to twenty minutes—minimum ten, maximum twenty—then go to sleep.

Feel the silence of the womb

Let silence become your meditation. Whenever you have time, just collapse in silence—and that is exactly what I mean: collapse—as if you are a small child in your mother's womb. Sit this way and then by and by you will start feeling that you want to put your head on the floor. Then put the head on the floor. Take the womb posture as the child remains curled up in the mother's womb and immediately you will feel the silence is coming, the same silence that was there in the mother's womb. Sitting in your bed, go under a blanket and curl up and remain there utterly still, doing nothing.

A few thoughts sometimes will come, let them pass—you be indifferent, not concerned at all: if they come, good; if they don't come, good. Don't fight, don't push them away. If you fight you will become disturbed, if you push them away, they will become persistent; if you don't want them, they will be very stubborn about going. You simply remain unconcerned, let them be there on the periphery as if traffic noise is there. And it is really a traffic noise, the brain traffic of millions of cells communicating with each other and energy moving and electricity jumping from one cell to another cell. It is just the humming of a great machine, so let it be there.

You become completely indifferent to it; it does not concern you, it is not your problem—somebody else's problem maybe, but not yours. What do you have to do with it? And you will be surprised—moments will come when the noise will disappear, and you will be left all alone.

Moving from the negative to the positive
Negativity is very natural. It should not be so, but it is, because every child passes through many negative moments. When he is brought up, everybody is telling him what to do, what not to do—as if he is nobody. He is a small, tiny weakling in the world of giants, and everybody is trying to manipulate him. Deep inside he goes on saying, "No, No, No!" On the outside he has to say, "Yes, yes, yes." He becomes a hypocrite.

So try this method each night for sixty minutes. For forty

minutes, just become negative—as negative as you can. Close the doors, put pillows around the room. Unhook the phone, and tell everybody that you are not to be disturbed for one hour. Put a notice on the door saying that for one hour you should be left totally alone. Make things as dim as possible. Put on some gloomy music, and feel dead. Sit there and feel negative. Repeat "No" as a mantra.

Imagine scenes of the past—when you were very dull and dead, and you wanted to commit suicide, and there was no zest to life—and exaggerate them. Create the whole situation around you. Your mind will distract you. It will say, "What are you doing? The night is so beautiful, and the moon is full!" Don't listen to the mind. Tell it that it can come later on, but that this time you are devoting completely to negativity. Be religiously negative, mm? Cry, weep, shout, scream, swear—whatsoever you feel like, but remember one thing—don't become happy! Don't allow any happiness. If you catch yourself, immediately give yourself a slap! Bring yourself back to negativity, and start beating the pillows, fighting with them, jumping. Be nasty! And you will find it very difficult to be negative for these forty minutes.

This is one of the basic laws of the mind—that whatsoever you do consciously, you cannot do. But do it—and when you do it consciously, you will feel a separation. You are doing it but still you are a witness; you are not lost in it. A distance arises, and that distance is tremendously beautiful. But I am not saying to create that distance. That is a by-product—you need not worry about it. After forty minutes suddenly jump out of the negativity.

Throw the pillows away, put on the lights, put on some beautiful music, and have a dance for twenty minutes. Just say "Yes! Yes! Yes!"—let it be your mantra. And then take a good shower. It will uproot all the negativity, and it will give you a new glimpse of saying yes.

This will cleanse you completely. Once these rocks are removed you will have a beautiful flow.

Laughing meditation

In the night before sleeping and in the morning try this meditation for ten to forty minutes. Sitting silently just create a giggle in your being, as if the whole body is giggling, laughing. Start swaying with the laughter—let it spread to your hands and your feet. If it comes uproariously, allow it; if it comes quietly, allow it. Let your whole body be involved—not just the lips and the throat, but rising up from the soles of your feet and then moving to the belly.

Visualize yourself as a small child. If you feel like it, start rolling on the floor. The noise is not so meaningful as the involvement. Don't remain stiff—relax, cooperate with it. Even if in the beginning you exaggerate it a little, it will be helpful.

Afterward lie down on the earth or the floor, facing the floor. Make contact with the earth, feel that the earth is your mother and you are the child—get lost in that feeling. Breathe with the earth, feel one with the earth. We come from the earth and one day we will go back to it.

After this time of contact with the earth, your dancing will have a different quality to it.

This is in the night before you go to sleep. Just ten minutes will do and then fall asleep. Again in the morning, the first thing—you can do it in your bed. So the last thing at night and the first thing in the morning. The night laughter will set a trend in your sleep. Your dreams will become more joyous, more uproarious, and they will help your morning laughter; they will create the background. The morning laughter will set the trend for the whole day. In the whole day, whenever there is an opportunity, don't miss—laugh.

Relieving tension in the face

Every night before you go to sleep, sit in your bed and start making faces—just as small children enjoy doing. Make all kinds of faces—good, bad, ugly, beautiful, so the whole face and the musculature start moving. Make sounds, nonsense sounds will do, and sway, just for ten to fifteen minutes and then go to sleep. In the morning before you take your bath, again stand before the mirror and for ten minutes make faces. Standing before the mirror will help more: you will be able to see and you will be able to respond.

In childhood many people have controlled the face too much. They have repressed all kinds of emotions. They have made their faces absolutely nonexpressive; nobody can judge from their face what their feelings are.

So in the night for ten minutes make faces, make sounds, and enjoy it just like a small child, and in the morning before the mirror, so you will become an expert. Within two or three months it will be completely gone.

Moving from the head to the heart

Shift from thinking to feeling. And the best way will be to start breathing from the heart.

In the day as many times as you remember, just take a deep breath; feel it hitting just in the middle of the chest. Feel as if the whole existence is pouring into you, into your heart exactly in the middle—not on the left, not on the right . . . exactly in the middle. That is where your heart center is.

It has nothing to do with the physical heart. It is a totally different thing; it belongs to the subtle body.

So breathe deeply, and whenever you do, do it at least five times—deep breath; take it in, fill the heart. Just feel it in the middle—that the existence is pouring through the heart: vitality, life, godliness, nature . . . everything pouring in.

And then exhale deeply, again from the heart, and feel you are pouring out that which has been given to you back into existence. Do it many times in the day.

And you will become more and more sensitive, more and more aware of many things. You will smell more, you will taste more, you will touch more, you will see more, you will hear more; everything will become intense. You will start feeling life really throbbing in you.

Relaxation

Just watch a child—he is relaxed, he is in a let-go. And it does not need much wisdom to relax; it is a simple art, because you already knew it when you were born; it is already there, it just has to be made active from its dormant position. It has to be provoked.

All methods of meditation are nothing but methods to help you to remember the art of let-go.

Simple principles have to be remembered. The body should be the beginning. Lying down on your bed, before sleep comes, start watching with closed eyes the energy from your feet. Move from there—just watch inside: Is there some tension somewhere? In the legs, in the thighs, in the stomach? Is there some strain, some tension? And if you find some tension somewhere, simply try to relax it. And don't move from that point unless you feel the relaxation has come.

Go through the hands—because your hands are your mind; they are connected with your mind. If your right hand is tense, the left side of your brain will be tense. If your left hand is tense, the right side of your brain will be tense. So first go through the hands—they are almost the branches of your mind—and then reach finally to the mind.

When the whole body is relaxed the mind is already 90 percent relaxed, because the body is nothing but extensions of the mind.

Then the 10 percent tension that is in your mind . . . simply watch it, and just by watching, the clouds will disappear. It will take a few days for you; it is a knack. And it will revive your childhood experience, when you were so relaxed.

Within a few days you will be able to catch the knack. And once you have known the secret—nobody can teach it to you, you will have to search within your own body—then even in the day, at any time, you can relax. And to be a master of relaxation is one of the most beautiful experiences in the world. It is the beginning of a great journey toward spirituality, because when you are completely in a let-go, you are no longer a body.

If your whole body is relaxed, you simply forget that you are a body. And in that forgetfulness of the body is the remembering of a new phenomenon that is hidden inside the body: your spiritual being.

Let-go is the way to know that you are not the body, but something eternal, immortal.

Look into your life, where you can find some natural experience of let-go. There are moments when you are swimming. If you are really a swimmer you can manage just to float, not to swim, and you will find tremendous let-go—just going with the river, not even making any movement against the current, becoming part of the current.

You have to gather experiences of let-go from different sources, and soon you will have the whole secret in your hands.

10

———

paradise regained

Many times sitting in your presence I am overwhelmed by a very childlike feeling. It seems so familiar, yet from a long time ago. Is this significant?

This great experiment through which you are passing here is basically to achieve your lost childhood again.

When I say "your lost childhood," I mean your innocence, your eyes full of wonder, knowing nothing, having nothing, but yet feeling yourself at the top of the world. Those golden moments of wonder, joy, no tension, no worry, no anxiety, have to be regained, rediscovered.

Of course the second childhood is far more valuable and significant than the first. In the first the innocence was there because of ignorance, so it was not pure and clear and in your possession; it was just a natural thing that happens to every childhood. The second childhood is your greatest achievement—it does not happen to all. The second childhood makes you innocent without ignorance, the second childhood comes through all kinds of experiences. It is mature, centered, ripe.

You should be blessed that you are feeling like that. The second childhood is just exactly the existential meaning of meditation, and from there on is the great pilgrimage of coming back home—which you have never really left, which is impossible to leave, because it is you. Wherever you will go, you will find yourself there.

There is only one essential being in you which will be everywhere with you, without any condition. Even if you are in hell it doesn't matter, it will be with you; if you are in heaven it doesn't matter, it will be with you.

To find that essential core of your being is on the one hand utter innocence, and on the other hand is the greatest wisdom that has ever existed on the earth.

So your body may be becoming old, but if you are learning ways of being silent and peaceful and meditative and loving, you will not grow old. You will remain as young and as fresh as early morning dewdrops shining in the beautiful sunrise, looking far more precious than any pearls.

You should be happy and rejoice in your childhood. This is what Jesus meant when he said again and again, "Unless you are born again . . ." Even Christians have not gotten the meaning of his statement. They think literally that "unless you are born again" means that first you will have to die, and then you will be born, and on the judgment day Jesus will take you into paradise. That is not the meaning of the man.

What he is saying is: unless you die right now as a personality and emerge as an innocent individuality, unscratched, unpolluted by the society and the people . . . This is your new birth, this is resurrection.

"I don't want your son, Ernie, swimming in our pool anymore," says Mrs. Meyer to her neighbor, Mrs. Jones.

"But what has my poor little Ernie done?" asks Mrs. Jones.

"He is constantly peeing in the pool," says Mrs. Meyer angrily.

"Don't be so hard on him," says Mrs. Jones, "all children of his age do that!"

"Maybe they do," says Mrs. Meyer, "but not from the diving board."

Childhood has its beauties, because it does not know the etiquette, the manners, and all kinds of crap. It is so simple and so innocent and so spontaneous.

A man walked into a bar and was amazed to see a dog sitting at a table with three men playing poker. The man went over and asked, "Can that dog really read his cards?"

"Sure he can," said one of the men. "But he's not much of a player. Whenever he draws a good hand he wags his tail!"

That is absolutely innocent . . . the poor dog cannot contain his joy.

Two cockroaches were munching delicacies on top of a garbage pile when one of them began telling of some new tenants in the nearby apartments.

"I hear," he said, "that their refrigerator is spotless, their floors are gleaming, and there is not a speck of dust in the whole place."

"Please, please," said the other cockroach, "not while I'm eating!"

Such bad news . . . !

It will be a tremendous revolution the day we start learning the languages of birds, of bees, of cockroaches. They all have their ways of communicating. But then the heart feels a little sadness, because we have not been able to learn even to communicate with human beings, and we have been here for millions of years. What kind of stupidity is this, that we don't know the whole humanity as belonging to us and we belonging to it? All that man has done is simply butchering, murdering, war. The same energy, the same effort would have made this world the greatest miracle in the whole universe.

But we don't understand each other. We may even be speaking the same language, but understanding is not necessarily expected; what is expected is misunderstanding. So people are hiding themselves, hiding their childhood, hiding their innocence, protecting themselves from everybody with defense measures; otherwise you will see children young and old all playing in this garden of the earth, rejoicing, laughing, giggling. Why this seriousness? Man has not gained anything out of this seriousness; he has simply lost everything—but he continues to be serious.

I am absolutely against seriousness.

I call it a psychological sickness.

Only a playful, childlike, innocent behavior is the right behavior, is what I would like to call virtuous behavior, religious, spiritual . . . not only human but divine.

The moment you are as innocent as a child you have transcended humanity, you have entered into the world of godliness.

I was never really a child when I was one, but these last few days, I often feel like a little child.

That's really a miracle, really a miracle! To feel like a child again is a great conversion. Allow it . . . don't feel shy about it. Put your age and mind aside. If you can, you will suddenly feel a new energy arising in your body. Your age will be reduced by at least twenty years. You can become younger immediately and you can live longer. So allow it; it is beautiful.

One has to become a child again and then life is complete. In childhood we start and in childhood we end. If one dies without becoming a child, his whole life circle is incomplete. He will have to be born again.

That is the whole Eastern idea of rebirth. If you can be reborn—reborn in this life—there is no need to be born again. If you can really become a child in this body, there is no need to be born into the world again. You can live in the heart of existence. There is no need then to come back. You have learned the lesson and completed the circle.

My whole effort is this: to help you to be a child again. It is difficult, it is very difficult, because your whole experience, your whole pattern, your whole character resists and says, "What are you doing? It looks foolish!" But be foolish and let it assert itself. You will feel so unburdened, so new. Allow it. This is something very significant, but you can lose it. If you don't help it, it can be lost easily because your whole personality will be against it. You will have to consciously work a way for it, to allow it. Your whole past will be there like a rock and this new phenomenon will just be like dripping water, a small stream, which can become a river if you help; otherwise the rock is too big. But ultimately, if one goes on helping, the softer, the more waterlike, the stronger one is, the more the rocklike things disappear.

In the long run the rock is always defeated by the water. The old man is always defeated by the child. Death is always defeated by life. One should remember that, and one should always help the softer, the younger, and fresher things.

Make friends with children and follow them around. Whatsoever they do, you do. They will enjoy it. Children are very receptive and they always understand. They will immediately understand that you look old but you are not. Just mix with children and forget about big people.

. . .

It is always good to go for a walk with a two-year-old or three-year-old child and to commune with him, to see what he is doing, to see how he walks and how he becomes interested in everything. A butterfly or a flower or a dog barking and the child is involved with each moment so totally. Only the child knows how to live, or when one again becomes a child, one knows how to live. In between there is only misery and hell.

So keep this idea of a three-year-old. Let that be your reality and your chronological age just a social phenomenon, just a facade. Just from the outside be grown-up; from the inside remain a child. And when you are alone, drop all your grown-upness; it is not needed. Behave like a child. And it will be good—play with small children.

Sometimes take them, go for a walk on the seashore or anywhere—in a garden—and just behave like them; don't force them to behave like you. Just follow them and you will find new insights arising in you.

Sometimes it will be frightening to feel like a child because then you become so vulnerable, so open, and anybody can hurt you. You become so helpless again . . . but that helplessness is beautiful. To be vulnerable is beautiful; to be hurt sometimes is beautiful. Just to avoid those hurts we become hard, we gather a crust, like steel, an armor. It is safe but it is dead.

You are in a really beautiful space! Remain in it, and invite it again and again.

Whenever you have an opportunity just become a child. In your bathroom, sitting in your tub, just be a child. Have all your toys around you!

osho international
meditation resort

Location: Located 100 miles southeast of Mumbai in the thriving modern city of Pune, India, the OSHO International Meditation Resort is a holiday destination with a difference. The Meditation Resort is spread over 40 acres of spectacular gardens in a gorgeous tree-lined residential area.

Uniqueness: Each year the meditation resort welcomes thousands of people from more than 100 countries. The unique campus provides an opportunity for a direct personal experience of a new way of living—with more awareness, relaxation, celebration and creativity. A great variety of around-the-clock and around-the-year program options are available. Doing nothing and just relaxing is one of them!

All programs are based on the OSHO vision of "Zorba the Buddha"—a qualitatively new kind of human being who is able *both* to participate creatively in everyday life *and* to relax into silence and meditation.

Meditations: A full daily schedule of meditations for every type of person includes methods that are active and passive, traditional and revolutionary, and in particular the OSHO Active Meditations™. The meditations take place in what must be the world's largest meditation hall, the Osho Auditorium.

Multiversity: Individual sessions, courses and workshops cover everything from creative arts to holistic health, personal transformation, relationship and life transition, work-as-meditation, esoteric sciences, and the "Zen" approach to sports and recreation. The secret of the Multiversity's success lies in the fact that all its programs are combined with meditation, supporting an understanding that as human beings we are far more than the sum of our parts.

Basho Spa: The luxurious Basho Spa provides for leisurely open-air swimming surrounded by trees and tropical green. The uniquely-styled, spacious Jacuzzi, the saunas, gym, tennis courts . . . all are enhanced by their stunningly beautiful setting.

Cuisine: A variety of different eating areas serve delicious Western, Asian and Indian vegetarian food—most of it organically grown especially for the meditation resort. Breads and cakes are baked in the resort's own bakery.

Night Life: There are many evening events to choose from—dancing being at the top of the list! Other activities include full-moon meditations beneath the stars, variety shows, music performances and meditations for daily life.

Or you can just enjoy meeting people at the Plaza Café, or walking in the nighttime serenity of the gardens of this fairy-tale environment.

Facilities: You can buy all your basic necessities and toiletries in the Galleria. The Multimedia Gallery sells a large range of OSHO media products. There is also a bank, a travel agency and a Cyber Café on-campus. For those who enjoy shopping, Pune provides all options, ranging from traditional and ethnic Indian products to all global brand-name stores.

Accommodation: You can choose to stay in the elegant rooms of the Osho Guesthouse, or for longer stays opt for one of the Living-In program packages. Additionally there is a plentiful variety of nearby hotels and serviced apartments.

www.osho.com/meditationresort

about osho

Osho defies categorization. His thousands of talks cover everything from the individual quest for meaning to the most urgent social and political issues facing society today. Osho's books are not written but are transcribed from audio and video recordings of his extemporaneous talks to international audiences. As he puts it, "So remember: whatever I am saying is not just for you . . . I am talking also for the future generations."

Osho has been described by the *Sunday Times* in London as one of the "1000 Makers of the 20th Century" and by American author Tom Robbins as "the most dangerous man since Jesus Christ." *Sunday Mid-Day* (India) has selected Osho as one of ten people—along with Gandhi, Nehru and Buddha—who have changed the destiny of India.

About his own work Osho has said that he is helping to create the conditions for the birth of a new kind of human being. He often characterizes this new human being as "Zorba the Buddha"—

capable both of enjoying the earthy pleasures of a Zorba the Greek and the silent serenity of a Gautama the Buddha.

Running like a thread through all aspects of Osho's talks and meditations is a vision that encompasses both the timeless wisdom of all ages past and the highest potential of today's (and tomorrow's) science and technology.

Osho is known for his revolutionary contribution to the science of inner transformation, with an approach to meditation that acknowledges the accelerated pace of contemporary life. His unique OSHO Active Meditations are designed to first release the accumulated stresses of body and mind, so that it is then easier to take an experience of stillness and thought-free relaxation into daily life.

Two autobiographical works by the author are available:
Autobiography of a Spiritually Incorrect Mystic
Glimpses of a Golden Childhood

for more information

www.OSHO.com

A comprehensive multi-language website including a magazine, OSHO Books, OSHO TALKS in audio and video formats, the OSHO Library text archive in English and Hindi and extensive information about OSHO Meditations. You will also find the program schedule of the OSHO Multiversity and information about the OSHO International Meditation Resort.

Website:
http://osho.com/allaboutosho
http://www.youtube.com/OSHOinternational
http://www.Twitter.com/OSHO
http://www.facebook.com/pages/OSHO.International
http://www.flickr.com/photos/oshointernational

To contact **OSHO International Foundation:**
www.osho.com/oshointernational
oshointernational@oshointernational.com

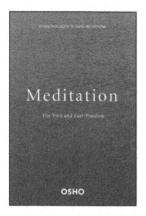

LIFE, LOVE, LAUGHTER: CELEBRATING YOUR EXISTENCE

In this collection of reflections, Osho's inspiring and loving stories go far beyond the usual chicken-soup fare. Osho mixes entertainment and inspiration, ancient Zen stories and contemporary jokes to help us find love, laughter, and ultimately, happiness. An original talk by Osho on DVD is included.

ISBN: 978-0-312-53109-6 • Paperback w/DVD
$14.95/$18.95 Can.

LOVE, FREEDOM, ALONENESS: THE KOAN OF RELATIONSHIPS

Love can only happen through freedom and in conjunction with a deep respect for ourselves and the other. Is it possible to be alone and not lonely? Where are the boundaries that define "lust" versus "love" and can lust ever grow into love? Osho offers unique, radical, and intelligent perspectives on these and other essential questions, as well as a golden opportunity to start afresh with ourselves, our relationships to others, and to find fulfillment and success for the individual and for society as a whole.

ISBN: 978-0-312-29162-4 • Paperback • $15.99/$18.50 Can.

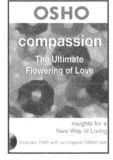

OSHO LIFE ESSENTIALS

The Osho Life Essentials series focuses on the most important questions in the life of the individual. Each volume contains timeless and always contemporary investigations into and discussions of questions vital to our personal search for meaning and purpose.

BELIEF, DOUBT, AND FANATICISM

Is It Essential to Have Something to Believe In?

978-0-312-59548-7

THE JOURNEY OF BEING HUMAN

Is It Possible to Find Real Happiness in Ordinary Life?

978-0-312-59547-0

DESTINY, FREEDOM, AND THE SOUL

What Is the Meaning of Life?

978-0-312-59543-2

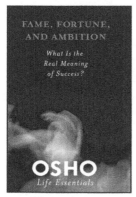

FAME, FORTUNE, AND AMBITION

What Is the Real Meaning of Success?

978-0-312-59544-9

INNOCENCE, KNOWLEDGE, AND WONDER

What Happened to the Sense of Wonder I Felt as a Child?

978-0-312-59545-6

POWER, POLITICS, AND CHANGE

What Can I Do to Help Make the World a Better Place?

978-0-312-59546-3

Please visit www.osho.com or www.stmartins.com/osho
for additional information on these titles.

ST. MARTIN'S GRIFFIN

Made in United States
North Haven, CT
30 May 2024

53102213R00157